The Lord's Horseman

You may have pictured in the England of the eighteenth century a moorland on a windy winter evening, and on the near horizon the glare of an ill-lit manufacturing town, and a single figure, small and slight, his long gray hair falling over his shoulders, sitting on a tired horse plodding forward with loosened rein. It is a subject the genius of a Millet might have made as memorable as his famous "Angelus."

F. J. FOAKES JACKSON
Social Life in England

UMPHREY LEE

THE LORD'S HORSEMAN

John Wesley the Man

ABINGDON PRESS

New York   Nashville

THE LORD'S HORSEMAN

SET UP, PRINTED, AND BOUND BY THE
PARTHENON PRESS, AT NASHVILLE,
TENNESSEE, UNITED STATES OF AMERICA

TO

Mary Margaret Lee

Preface

Jᴏʜɴ ᴡᴇsʟᴇʏ has never lacked for biographers. This is mainly, of course, because he was the founder of those Methodist churches which have become no inconsiderable part of present-day Protestantism. Most who know his name do not know that he ever did anything else, and they do not know that founding a church was something he did not want to do and for years declared he would never do.

The historians know that Wesley's influence extended far beyond the religious groups which emerged as a result of his work. Indeed, it has become fashionable to attribute to him much that has come into being in recent years: he has been claimed as the forerunner of liberal Protestantism, as the father of the social gospel, and as a Barthian born out of due season. Attractive as some of these attributions may be, it is historically sounder to see Wesley in the light of his century rather than in the light of theories which did not come to birth until he had been dead for a century. His wider influence may be studied in currents of his own time, in the humanitarian movement, in the growth of individualism, and, most of all, in evangelical Christianity both in the Church of England and among Dissenters.

Those who have taken in hand to write a life of Wesley have been many and of many sorts and conditions. Like all religious leaders he has sometimes been obscured by the incense smoke from the altars of devoted sons, and he has been analyzed by those who had every qualification to reassess historical figures except a knowledge of history. The biographies, good and bad, have been written by preachers, by professional biographers, by Methodists, by High Churchmen and Low Churchmen, by Roman Catholics, by historians, and by poets; and the end is not yet.

The only excuse for this book, when it was first written or now, is that it deals with Wesley the man in the light of Wesley's own century. Because he lived throughout most of the eighteenth century and wrote journals, diaries, letters, books, and pamphlets for nearly seventy years, Wesley left an almost unparalleled record of himself and of his times. And the times were stirring. The modern world was coming to birth, and the English were busy inventing spinning jennies and parliamentary government and trying to colonize the earth. Wesley himself was more than a founder and a historical source; he was one of the most interesting of men.

Although not technically a scholar he read everything that came to hand: scientific works, books of travel, fiction, political treatises, as well as religious books by Roman Catholic and Protestant alike. At times his *Journal* reads like the work of a book reviewer extraordinary to the eighteenth century. In addition to the ancient languages, which a clergyman was supposed to know, and French, which a gentleman was supposed to understand, Wesley could at least read German, Italian, and Spanish. He had never made the Grand Tour that young lords made, but he had been in America before George III was born, and he had tramped over a large part of the Germanies and Holland. As for the British Isles, Wesley knew them as did few Englishmen of his century.

Above all, Wesley knew and liked people, especially those whom he called "plain people." He would have nothing of the newfangled democratic political ideas which were popularized by the American Revolution, but he discovered the common man before anyone invented that supercilious term.

To the people—rich and poor, gentlemen and laborers—Wesley preached the love of God. He was not given to much talk about hell-fire, although he believed that God was the God of judgment as well as of pardon. His religion, he said when he was free of theological terminology, was the religion of love. And the common people heard him for more than half a century, sometimes sullenly, sometimes angrily, most of the time gladly.

In these days one needs to make no apology—except for his inability as an author—for writing the life of such a man. But in 1820 when the first biographer from the polite world, Robert Southey, poet laureate and biographer of Nelson, wrote his famous *Life,* he felt it necessary to explain his reasons for spending his time on such a man as Wesley. Wrote Southey: "The history of men who have been prime agents in those great moral and intellectual revolutions which from time to time take place among mankind, is not less important than that of statesmen and conquerors." And Southey was so daring as to predict that the time might come when the name of Wesley would be more generally known than that "of Frederic or of Catherine." That time came some time ago.

In the preparation of this edition I am under obligation to many people. I owe special thanks to my wife, who has helped me with the proofreading.

UMPHREY LEE

Contents

CHAPTER I

Out of the Fens

THE TRAVELER who jogs leisurely along the well-kept road between Haxey and Epworth in northern Lincolnshire will be pleased, if he is a thrifty soul, with the carefully tilled and fertile fields which lie between typical North Country English villages; but he will hardly suspect that a little more than a century ago this was part of "fen lands" where only an occasional hillock appeared above a sea of waters. The strip of land lying between the Trent, the Don, and the Idle rivers was until the nineteenth century well deserving of its ancient name, "The Isle of Axholme." During most of the year the Isle was inaccessible from the outside world except by boat, and the inhabitants made their scanty living by fishing and by cultivating such fields as lay above the yearly overflow. The land is everywhere low, at no place rising to more than two hundred feet above sea level; but there is now little indication of the swamps which once made the Isle a lonely and desolate waste.

The change in the character of the country is due to a system of drainage which was completed in the beginning of the last century. The work was enterprised almost two centuries before, but the people of the Isle, enraged at a proposal to drain their swamps, stubbornly fought every effort which was made by lord or king toward carrying out the elaborate schemes which Dutch engineers made first under the patronage of Charles I, later under Cromwell, and then under Charles II. The reader in the British Museum may still thumb a yellowed pamphlet in which John Lilburne, foremost radical of the early Commonwealth, pleaded the cause of the Isle; and to this day the sere and brittle pages with their turbulent Cromwellian paragraphs are eloquent of the feelings of the fen dwellers. During most of the seventeenth century the Isle was at war with the authorities. Isolated from the outside world and busy in repelling what they thought an invasion of their rights, the "Islonians," as they were called, were surly and inhospitable. As late as 1839 men could remember when the dwellers on the Isle had been "rude, uncivil, and envious to all others." Especially did they have an antipathy for Tory politicians and churchmen. Owing to the constitution of English local government, their curates and rectors had all too much to do with enforcing the authority which the people abhorred; and to the fen people the clergy were as the tax gatherers. The attitude of the Islonians toward the latter may be illustrated by the experience of Nathaniel Reading, appointed at the end of the seventeenth century to enforce the collection of taxes, who was compelled to fight no less than thirty-one pitched battles and then had his house burned for his pains.

The principal town of the Isle is Epworth. It is well situated, as such things go in the fen lands; an observer remarked, some four hundred years ago, that "Hepworth is the best uplandish town for building in one streate in the Isle." Only a century ago Epworth was a straggling town, which could be described as "pleasantly situated on the side of a hill." "Three streets lead into a small but neat and clean looking Market-Place," continues the description, "and that which comes from the west is in length considerably more than a mile, having here and there a good house standing apart, with a garden and small enclosure between." The town had a weekly market and a fair twice yearly. Until the end of the eighteenth century these markets and fairs were well patronized and Epworth was a prosperous village, but with the coming of steam navigation on the Trent, and with the later advent of the railroad into the Isle by way of Haxey, Epworth became a sleepy village, almost forgetful that it once belonged to the great house of Mowbray, and recalling its other glories only when visitors come to see the rectory and the old church on the hill.

The church of St. Andrew is the pride of the village. Into its walls are written the architectural history of the Isle, for the nave, the chancel, the north porch, the tower, are all of different periods. The tower is excellent, but of much later date than the nave; and the tired-looking aisle pillars, a little awry after their vigil of centuries, seem to be proudly unaware of the garish modernity of the Victorian window over the altar. In the churchyard gnarled old trees bend over crumbling tombstones, and flagstones lead away between other more stately trees toward the village. On the other side of the market is the rectory. The building, which stands now in a very respectable garden and behind most respectable walls, has been enlarged in recent years; but the main part of the old rectory was built in 1709. Before that time there was a smaller house "built all of timber and plaster, and covered with a straw thatch."

To this older rectory, one year after Nathaniel Reading's house had been burned by the inhabitants of Axholme, came a new rector and his wife. A little, keen-eyed, high-tempered man, the new rector of Epworth was of good family, the Wesleys or Wellesleys, of whom several had already made their mark in the kingdom. Indeed, beginning with the grandfather of the rector, one Bartholomew Wesley, who was ejected from his living in 1662 for nonconformity, and ending with the organist and composer Samuel Sebastian Wesley, who died in 1876, there is an unbroken line of famous sons of the family. Seven of them, in two centuries, are in the *Dictionary of National Biography*. Of these the Rev. Samuel Wesley, M.A., is one.

Samuel Wesley was born a gentleman and made himself a scholar. He had been brought up a dissenter and had been educated in a dissenting academy at Stoke Newington, where, along with Daniel Defoe, he received instruction from one Charles Morton, who was later to be vice-president of Harvard College in New England. Having decided to change his religion, Wesley entered Exeter College as a "poor scholar." He later served as chaplain on a man-of-war and as a London curate, and, at last, was given the living of Epworth, some say at the request of the dying Queen Mary. Samuel Wesley's chief claim to distinction among his contemporaries was, first, his scholarship and, second, his poetry. He had been one of the editors of *The Athenian Mercury,* that forerunner of *Notes and Queries,* which was edited by a friend and brother-in-law of Wesley, John Dunton, known mainly for his autobiography, *The Life and Errors.* As a poet Wesley had the honor of being criticized in most of the satires of his day. Garth in his *Dispensary,* Swift in the *Battle of the Books,* and later, Pope in the *Dunciad* paid their several respects to the little rector of Epworth. A poetical history of the Old and New Testaments was the rector's chief claim to literary distinction, and his *magnum opus* as a scholar was his *Dissertations on the Book of Job.* A copy of the latter was presented to Queen Caroline after the author's death. The queen smiled and said the binding was pretty.

Pope, in spite of his criticism of Samuel Wesley, a criticism which he carefully expunged from later editions of the *Dunciad,* felt kindly toward the rector. He spoke of him in carefully chosen words as a scholar and "an old Tory." Whether or not Wesley was a poet, he was certainly a Tory. He agreed with the great body of the Anglican clergy in contending for the highest theory of church privilege and in opposing Whig bishops. Wesley was for several terms one of the two representatives of the diocese of Lincoln to the lower house of Convocation, the legislative body of the Church of England, and there supported the lower house in its fight for independence from the dominantly Whig house of bishops.

The rector's wife was also of good family. The daughter of a distinguished dissenting clergyman, Samuel Annesley, one-time vicar of Milton's church, St. Giles, Cripplegate, Susannah Wesley was, like her husband, a convert to the Church of England. Of gentle blood—her father was nephew to the first Earl of Anglesey—and of unusually strong mind, Susannah Annesley had studied far beyond the mark set for women of her day; and she held her convictions, both theological and political, with a confidence born of both her character and her intellect.

These two came at last to live in the old rectory at Epworth, which looked out over the bleak landscape, all water in summer and all ice in winter. For eight years they attended to house and glebe and parish, and begat more sons and daughters. On June 17 (Old Style), 1703, John Wesley was born, second son and fifteenth child. His elder brother, Samuel, was thirteen, and almost ready to be sent to the great Westminster School, in London; Emilia, Susannah, Mary, and Hetty were the surviving sisters of the household. Three others of the rector's numerous brood were as yet unborn—Charles, Martha, and Kezziah.

When John was six years old, the rectory was burned; and he was barely saved by the effort of some neighbors. The rector, having given up his second son for lost, received him back as "a brand plucked out of the burning." He took the rescue as a sign that God intended great things for the boy. Whatever God intended, the purpose of the Epworthians was plain; for they had fired the house as part of their campaign against the rector, who had been unpopular since his induction into the living.

In the first place he was a clergyman and a Tory. In the second place he was a friend of Nathaniel Reading, attorney and collector of taxes. In the third place he was a strict disciplinarian, visiting his parish, inquiring into the private lives of his parishioners, and relentlessly enforcing ancient canons. So the resentful Islonians waged war upon him, stabbed his cattle, maimed his sheep, and fired his house.

The house was rebuilt in 1709 and still stands as a testimonial to the sturdy good taste of the rector. But for many years there was little furniture in it. During this time, when poverty kept the new rectory unfurnished, the family lived part of the year at the village of Wroote, which had been added to the living.

For six months of the year, sometimes for longer, the thatched parsonage at Wroote rose out of a world of waters, forlorn as a cornstack, and the Rector of Epworth journeyed between his two parishes by boat, often in soaked breeches, and sometimes with a napkin tied over his hat and wig.

The rector's poverty was partly a result of his genius for running into debt. While John was very small, some of Samuel Wesley's political enemies revenged themselves on him by having him imprisoned for three months in Lincoln Castle for his debts. Once the Archbishop of York questioned Mrs. Wesley as to whether she had ever actually wanted bread. "My Lord," answered Susannah, "strictly speaking, I never did want bread. But then I had so much care to get it before it was ate, and to pay for it after, as has often made it very unpleasant to me; and I think to have bread under such terms is the next degree of wretchedness to having none at all."

To pay his debts, Wesley had to resort to his patrons for aid. The Archbishop of York and the Duke of Buckingham came more than once to his rescue, and the little rector was duly grateful. Literary men were accustomed to accept help of this kind, and Samuel was nothing if not literary. But beyond the limits of respectable patronage he would not go. When the Archbishop proposed to make application to the House of Lords for a "brief"—that is, authority to take public collections—to relieve the clergyman and his numerous progeny, Wesley declined the offer, observing dryly that such an action would doubtless be "the first instance of a brief for losses by child-bearing which ever came before that honorable house."

Unable to associate with the villagers, whom they regarded as clods and worse, cut off from the great world by miles of sullen, turgid waters, living in poverty galling to their gentility, the Wesley household was a world unto itself. And the Wesley children bore to their graves marks of their isolation, of their confinement to the weary, monotonous fen lands, of their resentment of poverty and suffering. They were all more or less eccentric; at least four of the girls made unhappy marriages; one of them brought shame on the country rectory.

But their lot was not altogether melancholy. In their mother they had a domestic engineer of marvelous ability. While her fiery little husband disciplined the parish, wrote pamphlets against dissenters, or attended Convocation, Susannah taught her children to cry softly and to fear the rod. They were cared for in military fashion, each having his time and his duty. She taught them herself, teaching them the Lord's Prayer as soon as they could speak. After they were five, they were taught to read, one day being given to teaching the alphabet. Six hours of each day were spent in school, and at the evening the elder each took one of the younger and read to him the psalm and chapter for the day. Instruction was carried into higher branches, Mrs. Wesley even writing a system of theology for one of her daughters. The tract remains, witness alike to Susannah's understanding of current theological problems and to the dryness of that part of her teaching.

Under such rule John's mind flourished as in its native air, for he early disclosed an irrepressible and often exasperating logic. "Child," said his father one time, "you think to carry everything by dint of argument; but you will find how little is

19

ever done in the world by close reasoning." At another time
Samuel was provoked to anger by his offspring's methodical
mind. "I profess, sweetheart," he said to his wife, "I think our
Jack would not attend to the most pressing necessities of nature
unless he could give a reason for it."

Despite the monotony of life in Epworth, there was much
to stir the imagination and to fire the ambition of the Wesley
children. When John was four years old, his elder brother,
Samuel, entered as King's Scholar the Westminster School in
London, at that time one of the most famous in Europe because of its late headmaster, Busby. When John was eight,
Samuel entered Christ Church, Oxford. Three years later he
was called back to Westminster as usher. During his early boyhood, therefore, John was hearing from Samuel of life at Oxford and London and of happenings in the world of politics
and literature in which his father moved when he could get
away from his obscure parish.

Of politics the rector's children would certainly hear enough.
Before John's birth a political disagreement had been sufficient
to cause a temporary separation between the fiery little poet
and his determined spouse. "Sukey," said Samuel to his wife
during the last days of William III, "why did you not say 'Amen'
this morning to the prayer for the king?"

"Because," she said, "I do not believe the Prince of Orange
to be king."

"If that be the case," was the little man's reply, "you and
I must part; for if we have *two* kings, we must have *two beds.*"
Accordingly he went to his study, spent a little time there, and
rode off to London, where he was convocation man. "On March
eighth in the following year, 1702," so John Wesley later told
the story, "King William died; and as both my father and
mother were agreed as to the legitimacy of Queen Anne's title,
the cause of their misunderstanding ceased. My father returned

to Epworth, and conjugal harmony was restored once more."[1]

Before John was old enough to walk, his father was in no little trouble through the unauthorized printing of some letters that he had written on dissenting academies. When John was six years old, that is, in the year of the fire, Henry Sacheverell, a Tory firebrand, preached an inflammatory sermon in St. Paul's condemning toleration and advocating the highest doctrines of passive obedience. The sermon was declared seditious by the House of Commons, and Sacheverell was impeached. His defense was thought by some to have been on a literary and scholarly plane which his previous reputation had led no one to anticipate, and in later years John Wesley asserted that his father had written Sacheverell's defense. If this were so, the Epworth parsonage must have rung with the famous trial in which the Tory champion was convicted and suspended from preaching for three years; for the outcome of the trial was to arouse popular feeling to such an extent that, when Sacheverell made a tour of the country immediately afterward, he was received with acclaim far out of proportion to his merits. The whole incident was part of the bitter struggle between High Church and Low, and may well have left its mark upon the Lincolnshire boy whose High Church notions were to be long in dying.

In 1714 John was nominated by the Duke of Buckingham, his father's patron, to Charterhouse; and he went up to London in January to enter the famous school at which he was to spend the next six years. While there he was fagged unmercifully, for the older boys stole the meat of the smaller ones and allowed them only bread as their main dish. But young Wesley followed his father's advice, obediently ran thrice around the Charterhouse yard each morning, and thrived. Nor did his spirit suffer.

[1] Recently published letters show that Susannah consulted the nonjuring bishop George Hickes in her dilemma. John's dates were slightly wrong, but he was right about his mother's opinions. *Proceedings,* Wesley Historical Society, xxix, 3, pp. 50-57.

A well-founded tradition has it that an usher once found him haranguing a group of smaller boys and inquired of the orator why he chose to associate with lower-form boys rather than with older pupils. Young Wesley's reply was oracular: "Better to rule in hell than to serve in heaven."

While John was a student at Charterhouse, he heard with no little interest of strange happenings in the rectory at Epworth. During the winter of 1716–17 the rectory was disturbed by a mischievous spirit who knocked on walls, opened doors, banged the furniture, and in general made himself thoroughly unpleasant. Especially did the spirit abhor the Rector's loyal prayers; he was unusually demonstrative when that worthy prayed for the king. The girls named the ghost "Old Jeffrey" and learned that they could torment him by speaking disrespectfully of his activities, as by suggesting that the noises were caused by rats or mice. The rector attempted in every way to make the ghost speak, even remaining in an otherwise empty room to exhort the spirit to speak his mind, but to no avail.

The story was told at great length in letters to John, who later gathered all the material together into as entertaining a handful of letters as was ever written. His father, his mother, the girls, even a neighboring clergyman, wrote out their differing versions to John's delight. Already he was gathering material on points which aroused his interest. But there is no reason for thinking that this incident is responsible for John Wesley's undoubted credulity in later life. One has only to read certain pages of Boswell to know that the eighteenth century needed no incitement to believe in ghosts. For that matter, Old Jeffrey was so convincing a ghost that he was believed by a successor of Samuel Wesley to have returned a century later to plague the inhabitants of the Epworth rectory. Whether or not the ghost returned, a century later learned men were still arguing about him. In 1791 Joseph Priestley, the famous chemist, included the accounts of Old Jeffrey in his *Original Letters by the Rev.*

John Wesley. Priestley, however, could see no good end accomplished by the ghostly antics and concluded that they were produced by natural causes. In 1820 Robert Southey, poet laureate and biographer, thought that the manifestations might have been "preternatural" if not miraculous. The noises have been attributed to everyone from malevolent neighbors to the mischievous Hetty, but whoever was responsible, Old Jeffrey's epic remains one of the best ghost stories in history, and the little boy in Charterhouse must have shivered joyfully as he read the letters which his inquiries elicited and rejoiced in his father's loyal defiance of the Jacobite apparition.

For reasons more substantial than ghosts, the young student was living in stirring times; for the year 1715 had seen the uprising of the North in the cause of the Pretender. Young Wesley was in the midst of the ferment, for his brother Samuel, then usher at Westminster, was a close friend of Francis Atterbury, Bishop of Rochester and Dean of Westminster, who in 1723 was convicted of treason and banished. John Wesley always defended his elder brother against the charge of Jacobitism, asserting that Samuel was unswervingly loyal to the reigning house. Opponents pointed out not only Samuel's loyal attachment to Atterbury, but also his later diatribes against Sir Robert Walpole and his government, and, finally, a plain statement of Samuel's own daughter after her father's death. Perhaps the real state of Samuel's heart will never be known, but during the years in London, when the country was at fever heat at the thought of treason, the little boy in Charterhouse, already curious about everything alive, reveled in his brother's stories of great men and great events.

Many years afterward John remembered stories which his brother had told him—stories of men found naked on the cold steps of the King's Scholars at Westminster; of a thrilling rescue of a beautiful woman held prisoner by a mad physician; of the amours of Matthew Prior, poet. A part of this time John seems to have been the guest of his brother, for in 1719 Samuel wrote home that "Jack is with me, and a brave boy, learning Hebrew as fast as he can."

One may picture the second son of the poet of Epworth learning as fast as he could, but eagerly taking in other matters besides Hebrew characters. Methodist biographers are wont to deplore a letting down in the Wesley standard of piety at this time, for John wrote later that during his years at Charterhouse he

was much more negligent than before even of outward duties; and almost continually guilty of outward sins, which I knew to be such though they were not scandalous in the eyes of the world. However, I still read the Scriptures and said my prayers morning and evening.

The last sentence will perhaps save his reputation in the eyes of the less exacting, and a glimpse of Wesley as he left Charterhouse for Oxford, in 1720, may serve to assure the reader that the little boy who was "a brand plucked out of the burning," who wished, in Miltonic phrase, rather "to rule in hell than to serve in heaven," was on his predestined way.

Old Samuel Wesley was urgent that John visit Sacheverell and secure from him letters of recommendation. Accordingly John called on the venerable doctor. Wrote John in later years:

When I was introduced, I found him alone, as tall as a maypole and as fine as an archbishop. I was a very little fellow. . . . He said, "You are too young to go to the University; you cannot know Greek and Latin yet. Go back to school." I looked at him as David looked at Goliath, and despised him in my heart. I thought, "If I do not know Greek and Latin better than you, I ought to go back to school indeed." I left him, and neither entreaties nor commands could have again brought me back to him.

In June, 1720, at the age of seventeen young Wesley entered Christ Church, Oxford.

CHAPTER II

A Restless Collegian

THE OXFORD to which Wesley went up from Charter-house was not the clean, well-paved, decorous town of the twentieth century. Eighteenth-century Oxford had the ill-kept streets and slovenly houses which characterized other English towns of the period. But, as today, the sleepy gray city in the plains was distinguished by the tower of Christ's, the ancient walls of Merton, and the grove of Trinity; and the boy who came up to his elder brother's college on a June day in 1720 was so captured by the venerable university that ever afterward he was to look back with longing for an academic peace to which his own venturous spirit would not allow him to return.

The students of Oxford in the eighteenth century matricu-lated early, at sixteen or seventeen. Colleges filled with these youngsters were not known for their scholarship, although the fault doubtless lay more with the indifference of the instructors than with the age of the students. Christ Church and Lincoln seem to have preserved more of the air of learning than any other college in this period.

Christ Church, where young Wesley was matriculated, was conspicuous for its loyalty to the reigning house. Oxford, the headquarters of Charles I in civil-war days, was for a long while reputed to be Jacobite in sympathy; but Christ Church early accepted the Hanoverian succession, and the other colleges fol-lowed. Whatever their politics, all of them were united in their loyalty to the church. Excessive zeal might be frowned upon and too close observance of the canons suspect, but allegiance to the Establishment as a social necessity and a national symbol was nowhere more insisted upon than at the university. Within this courtesy of outward subscription there was room for theological wrangles and most lax observance of the ordinances. The university imagined itself loyal to the church at a time when within her colleges the church's doctrines were doubted and her order neglected.

Information as to Wesley's life as an undergraduate in a college where churchmanship was more valued than religion is very meager, but such material as is available indicates that he was a normal, somewhat careless youngster, dabbling in verse and taking kindly to outdoor life. Tennis and river sports seem to have bulked large in his scholastic program. In 1726 John sent his elder brother some specimens of his translations from the Latin. The theme of one was a bee which came to an untimely end after tasting the "fair Celinda's" lips. The second example of the young collegian's poetic genius was a metrical rendering of one of the Psalms. His verse was poor, but his taste was catholic.

Verse and the river did not exhaust Wesley's interests. Even more worldly abilities are reflected in the menu of a reunion dinner of old Charterhouse students of which Wesley was a steward in 1727. The menu is creditable as well to the ingenuity of the stewards as to the stomachs of the diners. The dinner included roasted pike, fried whitings, flounders, eels, shrimps, tongues, udders, pigeons, venison pasties, chines and turkeys, lamb and ragouts, wild fowls, sweetbreads and asparagus, almond tarts, roasted lobsters, pear tarts creamed, roast beef, fruit, jellies, custard, and florentines. The total cost of this dinner for eighty guests was £92 11s., of which sum the cook was paid £34, the wines cost £30 5s. 6d., and the musicians received £12 12s.

The cost of this dinner makes thoroughly understandable a

letter which Susannah Wesley wrote her son in 1724 asking if he had any reasonable hopes of being out of debt. She was most concerned for "the good, generous man" who had lent John ten pounds and had extended the loan until Susannah was ashamed to ask for further grace. She was expecting the return of a wealthy brother from India, a fancy which appears in several letters; but though the ship from India on which the brother was to have arrived came duly to port, the brother was not aboard, nor was he ever heard of again. In a later letter John's mother, writing from Wroote, advised him to save all the money he could conveniently spare, "not to spend on a visit"—she hastened to add—"but for a wiser and better purpose—to pay debts, and make yourself easy." The rector of Epworth corresponded with his son usually by brief, but pertinent, notes.

DEAR SON [he wrote on January 5, 1725],—Your brother will receive £5 for you next Saturday, if Mr. S— is paid the £10 he lent you; if not, I must go to H—, but I promise you I sha'n't forget that you are my son, if you do not that I am, Your loving father.

Samuel could be very businesslike about other people's debts, and he could also put a sting into his epistolary efforts, as the following attests:

Wroote, January 26, 1725

DEAR SON,—I am so well pleased with your decent behaviour, or at least, with your letters, that I hope I shall have no occasion to remember some things that are past. Since you have now, for some time, bit upon the bridle, I will take care hereafter to put a little honey upon it as oft as I am able; but then it shall be of my own mere motion, as the last £5 was; for I will bear no rival in my kingdom.

Your affectionate father,
SAMUEL WESLEY

But while the rector was giving his son advice in financial

matters, Emilia, the brilliant eldest daughter, was writing John that affairs were so bad with the rector's personal accounts that an Oxford undergraduate's extravagances could hardly make them worse.

I know not when we have had so good a year, both at Wroote and at Epworth, as this year; but instead of saving anything to clothe my sister or myself, we are just where we were. A noble crop has almost all gone, beside Epworth living, to pay some part of those infinite debts my father has run into, which are so many, . . . that were he to save £50 a year he would not be clear in the world this seven years. . . . One thing I warn you of: let not my giving you this account be any hindrance to your affairs. If you want assistance in any case, my father is as able to give it now as any time these last ten years, nor shall be ever the poorer for it.

For the time John seemed to be less disturbed than anyone else at his ability to follow in his father's footsteps. He wrote racy letters to his mother, retailing the gossip of the town. A gentleman of his acquaintance had been standing one night at the door of a coffeehouse when a thief jerked his wig and cap from his head, disappearing in the darkness. "I am pretty safe from such gentlemen," wrote John, "for unless they carried me away, carcass and all, they have but a poor purchase." Once the chief piece of news at the ancient seat of learning was that the famous highwayman Jack Sheppard had escaped from Newgate. Occasionally a ghost story which he had heard from a friend was included by a dutiful son anxious to please the parental ear. Aside from such items John gave considerable space to a new medical work he had read. The state of his health at this time gave him an interest in such things, and a famous book of the day, Cheyne's *Book of Health and Long Life,* recommended temperance and exercise, forbade highly seasoned meats, and advised drinking two pints of water and one pint of wine each twenty-four hours.

Wesley's careless and extravagant days were drawing to a

close in 1725, for with his undergraduate life almost over he was compelled to think of the future. Heretofore life in Oxford had been tolerable because seasoned with poetry, easily spent money, and outdoor sports; but only some new prospect could satisfy his voracious appetite for life. Naturally enough for a gentleman without estate, he thought of taking holy orders. His father discouraged him at first, preferring that his son follow "critical learning"; but his mother, with better understanding of his mind, advised "practical divinity." John had some scruples concerning the Athanasian Creed, but, having satisfied the authorities, he was ordained deacon by Bishop Potter on September 19, 1725.

At this time a fellowship in Lincoln College was vacated, and since the fellowship was reserved for natives of Lincoln, Wesley applied for it. His good reputation at Christ Church, together with his father's and elder brother's influence, helped him along; and in 1726 he was elected Fellow of Lincoln. His father's letters on receiving the news deserve remembrance:

Dear Mr. Fellow-Elect of Lincoln,—I have done more than I could for you. On your waiting on Dr. Morley [rector of Lincoln through whose influence, largely, Wesley was elected] with this he will pay you £12. You are inexpressibly obliged to that generous man.

And:

The last £12 pinched me so hard that I am forced to beg time of your brother Sam. till after harvest to pay him the £10 that you say he lent you. Nor shall I have so much as that (perhaps not £5) to keep my family till after harvest. I do not expect that I shall be able to do anything for Charles when he goes to the University. What will be my own fate, . . . God only knows. *Sed passi graviora.* Wherever I am, my Jack is Fellow of Lincoln.

With the income from his fellowship Wesley was for the first time financially independent. Residence at the university was required except in extraordinary cases, but the lax method of instruction insured little work. "When any person is chosen Fellow of a College, he immediately becomes a freeholder, and is settled for life in ease and plenty," wrote Nicholas Amherst of St. John's, in 1726. "He wastes the rest of his day," continued the same witness, "in luxury and idleness; he enjoys himself and is dead to the world; for a senior Fellow of a College lives and moulders away in a supine and regular course of eating, drinking, sleeping, and cheating the juniors." Such a prospect was in no way pleasing to as restless a spirit as Wesley. In the first place he wanted to proceed to his master's degree, which he did in 1727. In the next place he felt it necessary to help his old father as curate. He secured special leave from college, therefore, twice in the next three years and helped the old poet by preaching at Epworth and Wroote and serving occasionally as amanuensis on his *magnum opus,* which was growing to forbidding proportions in endless dissertations on Job.

For this period of Wesley's life the student has the advantage of diaries which were kept religiously. They were written in abbreviations, in shorthand, and in a cipher of Wesley's own invention. The early diaries give a faithful transcript of his daily—and hourly—activities. During his curacy, according to Curnock, editor of the standard edition of the *Journal,* Wesley

worked in the old garden at Wroot, made arbours (one of the seats in which probably remains in part to this day), gathered roses and elder flowers for his sisters, cut stakes, shot plovers in the fenland that then lay between the two parishes, wrote sermons for himself and his father, drank tea here and there, swam on summer mornings in the fen river, and went to every village fair within reach; . . . read and collected [that is, outlined] Spenser's *Faërie Queene,* indulged in *The Spectator,* in plays and other light literature; discussed points of doctrine or moral philosophy with his learned mother, carefully noting her opinions in his Diary; laboriously copied out *Dissertations on Job* for his father; read to his sisters as they sat working in the arbour, stood godfather to sister Nancy's baby, discoursed to Miss Kitty Hargreaves [a neighbor], read Spenser to her, and was not unappreciative of her gentle friendship as was his father (not his mother); . . . preached severely to the people of Epworth, . . . visited their sick, and buried their dead.

The picture is that of a well-bred young country clergyman, interested in the souls of his parishioners, but not unmindful of his own soul—and body. Further evidence of the curate's mundane interests is found in his correspondence of these days. A college mate, who probably wanted Wesley for a brother-in-law, wrote of his "most deserving, queer character," his "worthy personal accomplishments," his "noble endowments of mind," his "little and handsome person" and "obliging and desirable conversation." At the time Wesley was carrying on a stately correspondence with the daughter of the rector of Stanton, a village not far from Oxford. The young lady, after the fashion of such matters in that period, was styled "Varanese." There are few memorials of this first attachment, but a letter remains describing a visit of Wesley to Stanton. Such phrases as "on this spot she sat," "along this path she walked," "here she showed that lovely instance of condescension," adorn the account.

Wesley's acquaintance at the Stanton rectory led to another affair, this time with Mrs. Pendarves, later famous as Mrs. Delany, intimate friend of George III and his queen. This eminent lady, who in her youth was a friend and correspondent of Dean Swift and in her old age introduced Miss Burney to court, was a widow at the time she met young Wesley. In her correspondence with him she was "Aspasia," he was "Cyrus." It must be admitted that in such writing the curate was not at his best. His knowledge of courts and fine society was secondhand, and one example of his sophomoric style will explain why Mrs. Pendarves eventually tired of her correspondent:

31

I spent some very agreeable moments last night in musing on this delightful subject, and thinking to how little disadvantage Aspasia or Selima [Mrs. Pendarves' sister] would have appeared even in that faint light which the moon glimmering through the trees poured on that part of our garden where I was walking! how little would the eyes of the mind that surveyed them have missed the absent sun! what darkness could have obscured gentleness, courtesy, humility, could have shaded the image of God? Sure none but that which shall never dare to approach them; none but vice, which shall ever be far away!

It was possibly at this time that he and his father had their only real difference. One of the daughters had brought shame upon the Epworth household, and the rector's rage was terrible. The mother was for mercy, but the father was relentless and would have driven the luckless girl—Hetty it was—from the rectory. At this juncture John is said to have preached a sermon "On the Charity due to Wicked Persons." Sir Arthur Quiller-Couch's reconstruction of the story in his novel *Hetty Wesley* is fanciful and unfair to Samuel Wesley, but John's sermon doubtless did much to soften the family indignation, although it did not prevent Hetty from carrying out her rash vow to accept the first man who proposed.

By this time Wesley had made acquaintance with the work of the great devotional writer William Law, whose *Christian Perfection* had just been printed. Law quickened, if he did not awaken, Wesley's master passion, the pursuit of "holiness"— first for himself and then for others. At first John tried to introduce Law's discipline into the Epworth household, making even his calm-tempered mother angry. "Shall I be taught by a boy?" she cried; and the rector ordered his son "to get out of the house with his apostolical nostrums." There is no evidence that there was any definite break, but a family of self-willed Wesleys was no place for John to practice his new calling of spiritual director.

In 1729 Wesley was recalled to Oxford. There he pursued his work as Greek lecturer and lecturer in philosophy and logic. As a teacher he acquired a reputation for faithfulness and thoroughness which was unusual among early eighteenth-century dons, but other than academic interests were growing upon him. Charles had come up to Oxford from Westminster, where he had been under his brother Samuel's care. Like his elder brothers, Charles had entered Christ Church and had been a carefree, poetical student; but while John was curate at Wroote, Charles had fallen in with more serious students and had begun an informal club which met for study and devotion. To this group John joined himself when he returned to Oxford and because of his age and learning—and his masterful personality —soon became the leader. The club over which John now presided was to become one of the most famous in modern religious history.

Charles Wesley, the founder, had been in closer touch with his elder brother, Samuel, than had John. During the years when Samuel had so faithfully maintained his loyalty to Atterbury, Charles had been in his brother's house. There all the rigid, High Church notions to which Samuel was committed became a part of Charles's mental furniture. He came to Christ Church, therefore, not only fortified by his brother's careful tutoring in the classics, but predisposed to a high view of the church. He was also eccentric, as became a poet and a Wesley. When the fine frenzy was upon him, he would burst into his brother's neat room and, rapt in his composition, walk quite over John, table, books, and all.

Another of the company was George Whitefield, who was entered servitor at Pembroke, formerly a tapster in his mother's tavern at Gloucester. He had distinguished himself at the school of St. Mary de Crypt, in Gloucester, mainly for his acting in plays fostered by the school. His work in Oxford had been good, although he was handicapped by his poverty. When first at Oxford, he had been inclined to dissipation, but turning toward more serious thoughts, he had become acquainted with Charles Wesley and had joined himself to the little club. Benjamin Ingham, who also belonged to the club, was a man of some property. He was of Queen's and was destined to be a close friend of the Wesleys. In later years he left the Church of England and identified himself with the Moravians in Yorkshire. As more will be said in these pages about both Whitefield and Ingham, they may be dismissed here. The following notices, by indicating their later history, will show the quality of the men whom John Wesley led in Oxford.

James Hervey, who entered Lincoln in 1731, became one of the most popular religious writers of the eighteenth century. He fed the nascent romantic taste of the century with a lugubrious composition called *Meditations Among the Tombs,* which, bound with its companion piece, *Reflections on a Flower Garden,* went through seventeen editions in as many years and netted the author seven hundred pounds in royalties, no insignificant sum in those days. His printer was Samuel Richardson, the novelist; and the first success was followed by several other popular works, chief among which was *Theron and Aspasio,* calvinistic theology diluted with romantic scenery. This work sold nine thousand copies in two editions, evidence both of the perverted taste of the period and of Hervey's ability to satisfy it.

John Clayton, another member of the group, from Brasenose College, was from Manchester. He was a High Churchman of High Churchmen and closely associated with the nonjuring bishop Dr. Deacon, whose son was hanged for his part in the Jacobite uprising in 1745. Clayton was thought to have been private chaplain to the Young Pretender and was a fellow of the Collegiate Church of Manchester when he died. John Gambold, a Welshman, was entered servitor in Christ Church. Like the others, he became a clergyman of the Church of England;

but he later joined the Moravians and became one of their bishops. He edited their first English hymnbook, published in 1754.

Of other men connected with the club, one was Thomas Broughton, who served thirty-four years as secretary to the Society for the Promotion of Christian Knowledge; another was Charles Kinchin, who became dean of Corpus Christi College, and another was Richard Hutchins, later D.D., who became rector of Lincoln.

These were some of the men who composed the club which John Wesley dominated at Lincoln. "Mr. John Wesley was always the chief manager, for which he was very fit," wrote John Gambold. And he added:

He had, I think, something of authority in his countenance; though as he did not want address, he could soften his manner, and point it as occasion required. Yet he never assumed anything to himself above his companions; any of them might speak their mind, and their words were as strictly regarded by him as his were by them.

The club first of all set itself under the direction of John Wesley to obey the regulations of the colleges. John had made a reputation for conscientious performance of his own duties as lecturer and tutor, and he encouraged his friends to follow their studies and religious duties with the same assiduity. The little band attended divine service whenever possible and partook of the Lord's Supper every Sunday. In addition they met in John Wesley's rooms at Lincoln at regular hours for devotion and to hear their leader read from some chosen book. Careful study was given to the New Testament, possibly in the new Greek edition of Bentley. Beside their club meetings and university duties, the members visited the sick and prisoners, preaching especially to the latter, and organized classes for poor children. They used both their own savings and money solicited from their friends to relieve distress and occasionally to purchase freedom for some worthy man imprisoned for debt.

These practices were all regulated, under John's leadership, in the most methodical manner. Nor were their outward duties alone subject to punctilious orderliness. The private lives of the members were also ordered in the most scrupulous way. Early rising was counted an important virtue, and the day was divided carefully between study, pious exercises, and charity. Each day was ended with painful self-examination, and on Saturday the activities of the week were reviewed, sins carefully noted, and resolutions of better conduct dutifully made.

A part of one of Wesley's weekly examinations will illustrate the introspective discipline to which the members of the club subjected themselves. Wesley's record consists of questions which he addressed to himself and the resolutions which he made to cure defects. "Have I loved women or company more than God?" is his first question. The resolution which follows shows the nature of the offense which elicited this question. "*Resolve:* Never to let sleep or company hinder me from going to prayers." Another question was "Pride?" The Wesleys could use help against this sin, and Wesley notes as the remedy: "Consider death, the Scriptures." Often in his diary Wesley accused himself of idleness. This idleness consisted in reading light literature, such as the *History of Pyrates* (probably Captain Charles Johnson's *A General History of the Pirates,* printed in 1726), or in daydreaming. To remedy this, Wesley resolved to spend six hours a day in study. To cure "intemperate sleep," he would rise at five. To prevent unclean thoughts, he would remember "God's omnipresence."

The club was High Church in principles. The members spoke of the Communion as a "sacrifice," were convinced that baptism regenerated the subject, and talked of "confession." These opinions may have been influenced by men like William Law and Thomas Deacon, but it must be remembered that Samuel

Wesley was proud of his High Churchmanship, and Susannah, as was noted above, was sympathetic, at least until the accession of Queen Anne, with the nonjuring extremists.

The sight of a little group of men from several colleges—servitors, first-year men, tutors, and fellows—meeting together at regular hours for long study and devotion, or marching together to early sacramental services; some of them wearing their hair long, as John did, to save money; giving away all they could get; preserving puritanic abstinence from even innocent pleasures; and not hesitating to rebuke all who differed from them—this spectacle could not fail to excite ribald comment. The little company was dubbed "Bible Moths," the "Holy Club," the "Godly Club," and at last "Methodists." The name, which had been used in the seventeenth century to designate methodical people, was quickly taken up; and Methodists the followers of John Wesley remain to this day.

The opposition was supported by indolent fellows who disliked having their lax methods criticized and by calm, balanced scholars who suspected anything which smacked of fanaticism. George Whitefield later confessed that, when he first joined the club, he was ashamed to be seen knocking on Wesley's door. In 1732 an article in a weekly paper attacked the Methodists, accusing them of "enthusiasm" and hypocrisy. They were "the sorrowful brethren," enemies of all decency and restraint. But the Methodists were little disturbed. They endured this obloquy, perhaps enjoying the feeling of martyrdom which is the luxury of the young and the obsession of the fanatic. They took it for granted that offenses would come and counted it to their glory that they stood out from the crowd. "You must be singular or be damned," said their leader; and the Methodists were both singular and heartily damned by the rest of the university.

The "Holy Club" monopolized Wesley's interest for the time. Here he could expend his energies in exploring his own soul and in directing his fellows. Mrs. Pendarves tried to renew the correspondence which she had allowed to lapse after Wesley had come dangerously near a proposal. Wesley's preoccupied answer to her ingratiating letter was sufficient to cool any ardor she may have had for him. He wrote:

As for me, you do me no injury by your silence. It did indeed deprive me of much pleasure, and of a pleasure from which I ought to have received much improvement. But still, as it was one which I had no title to but your goodness, to withdraw it was no injustice.

Wesley was now studying with redoubled vigor. He was ordained priest in 1728, and his reading during the six months following included a formidable list:

Drake and Le Clerc's Physics, Burnet of the Reformation, Dennis against Pope, Salmon's Review, Welstead's Poems, Lee against Locke, Hickes of Schism, The Great Atlas, Dr. Halley of Magnetism and Gravity, Ditton of Matter's Thinking, the Souls of Brutes, Watts, Keil's Principia, Cowley, Locke, Norris, Heautontimorumenos, Cheyne of Fevers, Ezra in Hebrew, Horace's Odes, Horace's Epodes and Satires, Life of Whiteways, Horace de Arte Poetica and Epistles, St. Matthew, part of the 15th chapter of Proverbs (which he translated into Latin verse), Virgil's Eclogues, Logic, Virgil's Georgics, St. Mark, St. Luke, the Æneid, Life of Plutarch, Epictetus, the Acts, the Iliad, Romans, Xenophon, Colossians and Thessalonians, Proverbs and Ecclesiastes, Cornelius Nepos, Jackson, Cowley and Watts, On the Case of Subscribing, Prior and Berkeley, Satires of Juvenal, Vertôt's Revolutions of Rome, Synge on Toleration, Clarendon, Milton, Rapin on Eloquence, Ephesians, and twelve Odes of Anacreon.

When to this reading is added a correspondence so large that he had to give at least one day a week to it, the picture of John Wesley's first activities as a Methodist is complete. In such constant exercise, looking after his club, studying for his own profit and that of his students, directing inquiring minds by interminable correspondence, even his tireless genius found ample employment. But he was not to remain long undisturbed in his Oxford seclusion.

The old rector of Epworth was coming to the end of his days, working feverishly at his book in order that *Job* might be completed before he died. Death, he said, had already shaken him by the hand and would soon claim him altogether. There was another concern on the old man's mind. He wanted to see one of his sons settled in the living at Epworth, in order that his own ministry of four decades might be carried on and in order that Susannah might have a home. Samuel, who was now settled as headmaster of Blundell's School at Tiverton, in Devon, could not come; and both father and eldest son agreed that John was the one for the place. The rector believed that the living could be obtained for John if he would consent, so the matter was broached to the head of the Methodist Club. The living was a good one, two hundred pounds; and John and his mother, free from Samuel's extravagance, would have no need to worry about financial matters. John's reply to his father's request was wordy and thoroughly academic, thinly rationalizing John's preference of Oxford to the fen lands. He believed, he said, "that course of life tends most to the glory of God, wherein we can most promote holiness in ourselves and others." Oxford offered greater advantages for the cultivation of his own soul; his friends were there, and there he could have such "retirement" as was needful for his spiritual health. As for the old man's anxiety for his flock, John gave him eloquent comfort:

For yourself, I doubt not, but when your warfare is accomplished, when you are made perfect through sufferings, you shall come to your grave, not with sorrow, but as a ripe shock of corn, full of years and victories. And He that took care of the poor sheep before you was born will not forget them when you are dead.

Samuel, from Tiverton, joined his voice to his father's, but after a verbose controversy summed up the matter with the observation that none could move John's mind but He who made it.

It would seem that after his father's death John relented and made some halfhearted move to obtain the Epworth living, but, no doubt to his intense satisfaction, Epworth was disposed of to another petitioner. At any rate John had made clear to all that Lincolnshire had no attraction for him.

Another call, the romance of which he was not to resist successfully, was in readiness for him even then. In 1732 Colonel James Edward Oglethorpe, who had distinguished himself on the Continent as a soldier and at home as an apostle of prison reform, undertook the organization of a new American colony. In Georgia, Oglethorpe planned to provide a home for imprisoned debtors and other unfortunates. A board of trustees was formed, among whom was the first Earl of Egmont. Oglethorpe was acquainted with the Wesleys at least as early as 1728 when Samuel, Jr., addressed an ode to him in praise of his prison-reform work. The old rector had taken keen interest in the colonization scheme and had written Oglethorpe in the interest of his son-in-law, whom Samuel Wesley would have sent as a missionary to the Indians. If he had been younger, he said, he would have gone himself.

A former schoolmate of John was also one of the Georgia trustees, and he suggested that the Oxford Methodists would make suitable missionaries among undisciplined colonists in a new country. Dr. Burton, the trustee, had a lengthy correspondence with John concerning the project. At last John consented to go, believing that Georgia offered more opportunities for the cultivation of his spirit than Oxford. His chief motive in going to Georgia, he wrote on October 10, 1735, was the hope of saving his own soul. He hoped to learn the true sense of the gospel by preaching it to the heathen. The Indians had no corroding civilization to stand in the way of their understanding. Besides, in the idyllic environment of America he would have unlimited opportunity to mortify the flesh, especially his curiosity, by living like the children of nature on "water and the fruits of the earth."

In addition to John, who had the income from his fellowship, the trustees agreed to accept the services of another of the Oxford group, Benjamin Ingham, who also had an independent income. With the two missionaries who had money of their own the trustees hired Charles to act as secretary for Oglethorpe and even persuaded the Society for the Propagation of the Gospel in Foreign Parts to pay John fifty pounds additional. These matters arranged, the worthy gentlemen rested content that they had driven a good bargain for the Lord and the colony of Georgia.

CHAPTER III

With Oglethorpe in Georgia

O N SEPTEMBER 24, 1735, Lord Egmont and the other Georgia trustees spent an evening with the two Wesleys and Benjamin Ingham. The fact that these gentlemen were resolved to adventure into the new colony "to help the cause of religion" was set down by the trustees as "a particular providence and mark of God's favour" to the designs of the promoters. Three weeks later Wesley, his brother Charles, and Ingham went on board the "Simmonds" at Gravesend.

The "Simmonds" was a ship of 250 tons and was to be Oglethorpe's flagship. There were 112 colonists on board and 19 members of the crew. Of the colonists 26 were Moravians, German emigrants going to Georgia as religious refugees. With the "Simmonds" went the "London Merchant," with H. M. Sloop "Hawk" as escort. Contrary winds and the delay of the sloop kept the convoy at Cowes in the Isle of Wight until the tenth of December. But the missionaries were already at work.

The instructions of the Society for the Propagation of the Gospel to its ministers were that they should at once begin instructing and reproving their charges. Accordingly the trustees, shortly after Wesley went aboard, had a report that "Mr. Westley with the other clergymen were very zealous in discoursing them on religious subjects." Turning to Wesley's *Journal*, one can see how zealous the new missionaries were.

Having reduced their diet chiefly to rice and biscuits, the

Wesleys divided out their time—and the time of the other passengers—in good Oxford Methodist fashion:

Our common way of living was this: From four in the morning till five each of us used private prayer. From five till seven we read the Bible together, carefully comparing it (that we might not lean to our own understandings) with the writings of the earliest ages. At seven we breakfasted. At eight were the public prayers, at which were present usually between thirty or forty of our eighty passengers. From nine to twelve I commonly learned German, and Mr. Delamotte Greek. My brother writ sermons, and Mr. Ingham read some treatise of divinity or instructed the children. At twelve we met to give an account to one another what we had done since our last meeting, and what we designed to do before our next. About one we dined. The time from dinner till four we spent with the people partly in public reading, partly in reading to those whom each of us had taken in charge, or in speaking to them severally, as need required. At four were the evening prayers, when either the Second Lesson was explained—as it always was in the morning—or the children were catechized and instructed before the congregation. From five to six we again used private prayer. From six to seven I read in our cabin to two or three of the passengers, of whom there were about eighty English on board, and each of my brethren to a few more in theirs. At seven I joined with the Germans in their public service, while Mr. Ingham was reading between the decks to as many as desired to hear. At eight we met again, to exhort and instruct one another. Between nine and ten we went to bed, where neither the roaring of the sea nor the motion of the ship could take away the refreshing sleep which God gave us.

The first result of this "regular" manner of living was a complaint from a gentleman, son of a former governor of South Carolina, who said that the prayers in the public cabin were a great inconvenience to him. "He said he could not bear to stay in the room when so many people were in it and that he could not stay out of it while they were there for fear of catching cold." A compromise was effected whereby morning prayers were held while the gentleman was in bed, and the afternoon prayers were read between decks. Nothing was said as to how those who were not gentlemen felt about the arrangement.

A regular mode of living did not satisfy the Oxford Methodists, so they drew up a formal agreement pledging themselves to three things: (1) that none would undertake anything of importance without first proposing it to the others, (2) that one of them would submit to the judgment of the others, and (3) that in case of a tie vote the matter would be decided by lot. These resolutions, signed by the Wesleys, Ingham, and Charles Delamotte, son of a London sugar merchant, who was going along out of loyalty to John, were essential to the Wesleys' scheme of things. To this principle they remained loyal, even in matters of the heart, for more than a decade.

According to Ingham, Oglethorpe was "a pattern of fatherly care and tender compassion, being always ready, night and day, to give up his own ease and conveniences to serve the poorest body among the people." An instance of charity on the soldier's part was that he gave up his cabin to a Mrs. Welch, who was about to be delivered of a child and was seriously ill. Wesley gave her Holy Communion, and she immediately began to recover, making a safe delivery. Wesley was not through with Mrs. Welch, but for the present he turned his attention to other matters. The following statements in the *Journal* are the entries of a zealous pastor who was also a bachelor of little experience with women:

Dec. 27. I endeavoured to reconcile Mrs. Moore and Mrs. Lawley with Mrs. Hawkins, with whom they had had a sharp quarrel. I thought it was effected; but the next day showed the contrary, both Mrs. Moore, Mrs. Lawley, and their husbands being so angry with me, that they resolved (and prevailed on some others to do the same) never to be at prayers more.

. . . .

Dec. 30. Being informed Mrs. Lawley was ill, I hoped she might be in a milder temper, and therefore spent some time with her, and told her of the alteration of her behaviour since her being acquainted with Mrs. Moore.

An ocean voyage in 1735 in a ship of 250 tons was not a holiday excursion. This particular voyage lasted from December 10 until February 5, and the travelers had the experience of at least three violent storms. John was not sick during the voyage and spent his time, when he was not occupied with his interminable religious exercises, in observing and recording the events of life on shipboard. His conduct during the storms must be appraised with the fact in mind that he had a great fear of the sea, a fear perhaps carried over from his boyhood amid the forbidding waters of the Isle of Axholme.

The third storm Wesley described as the most violent of all:

"The waves of the sea were mighty, and raged horribly. They rose up to the heavens above, and clave down to hell beneath." The winds roared round about us, and—what I never heard before —whistled as distinctly as if it had been a human voice. The ship not only rocked to and fro with the utmost violence, but shook and jarred with so unequal, grating a motion, that one could not but with great difficulty keep one's hold of anything, or stand a moment without it. Every ten minutes came a shock against the stern or side of the ship, which one would think should dash the planks in a thousand pieces. In the height of the storm, a child, privately baptized before, was brought to be publicly received into the Church. . . . At seven I went to the Germans. I had long before observed the great seriousness of their behaviour. . . . There was now an opportunity of trying whether they were delivered from the spirit of fear, as well as from that of pride, anger, and revenge. In the midst of the psalm wherewith their service began, wherein we were mentioning the power of God, the sea broke over, split the mainsail in pieces, covered the ship, and poured in between the decks, as if the great deep had already swallowed us up. A terrible screaming began among the English. The Germans looked up, and

without intermission calmly sang on. I asked one of them afterwards, "Was you not afraid?" He answered, "I thank God, no." I
asked, "But were not your women and children afraid?" He replied mildly, "No, our women and children are not afraid to die."
From them I went to their crying, trembling neighbours, and
found myself enabled to speak with them in boldness and to point
out to them the difference in the hour of trial between him that
feareth God and him that feareth Him not. At twelve the wind
fell. This was the most glorious day which I had hitherto seen.

The man whose natural fear could not withstand his curiosity
as to the length of the interval between the big waves and whose
religious interests made this a "glorious" day was no ordinary
clerical meddler.

On February 4, almost two months from the day of departure
from Cowes, the "Simmonds" came within sight of land. In
the evening lesson were the words, carefully noted by the missionaries, "A great door and effectual is opened." The next day
the ships came into the Savannah River.

The new colony of Georgia lay between the Carolinas on
the north and Spanish Florida on the south. The one was jealous
and the cause of constant trouble as a commercial rival; the
other was always a menace, since England and Spain were on
the verge of hostilities. The settlements in Georgia were almost
all along the coast line from Savannah to St. Simon's Island,
a distance of about one hundred miles. Savannah was a non-
descript village on a bluff overlooking the river. There were
some two hundred houses in the town, and in 1737 Wesley
counted 518 inhabitants. The town was surrounded with strips
of white sand, wood, pine barren, and a swamp. On St. Simon's
Island was a new settlement called Frederica, built on a bluff
and in the midst of savannas and woods. Various emigrant settlements of Scots and Salzburgers were scattered about, twenty
to twenty-five miles from the main towns. The alternation of
scrubby pineland, swamps, and marshes, lying in the edge of

a great wilderness, made strange land for the debtors, ruined gentlemen, sturdy Scots, and pious Germans who came to the new colony, and yet stranger for the clergymen who came to minister to them.

John Wesley had come hoping to be a missionary to the Indians, but he had agreed to take care of the parish of Savannah until a new minister could be sent out. In the meantime he was concerned to learn all he could about the people among whom he hoped eventually to preach. A few days after the arrival of the convoy Wesley had his curiosity gratified by an interview with a famous Indian chief. This chief, Tomo-chachi, whom Oglethorpe had taken to England a few years before, came with his wife, a nephew, and a native whom Wesley called the "king" of the Savannah nation. The king dressed the part, with his face stained red in several places, his hair ornamented with beads, a scarlet feather over his ear, and a blanket for a parade uniform. Tomo-chachi's wife brought a jar of milk and one of honey, and expressed the wish that the white priests would feed the Indians with milk, for they were children, and be sweet as honey to them.

It was all as if out of a storybook, and Wesley's minute account testifies to his appreciation; but he is no less honest in recording the plain and thoroughly practical remarks of Tomo-chachi. When he was in England, said the chief, he really wanted the missionaries to come; but he and his people had been disillusioned. The French and Spaniards were building forts, and the English traders were liars. Nevertheless, he was glad to have the priests; he hoped his wise men would hear them. But his people did not want to be converted as the Spanish converted; they wanted instruction.

Thus began Wesley's ministry in America. During the course of it he was forced to go often to settlements outside of Savannah, and his means of traveling was walking or riding in a flat-bottomed barge, a rough vessel in troubled waters. Once he fell asleep on deck to wake up under water, having rolled over-board in his sleep. At another time, walking with Delamotte and a guide to an inland settlement, he was lost; and after wading swamps breast deep, he and his companions slept on the cold ground without a fire. His own love of outdoors, in spite of his natural physical frailty, carried him through his Georgia labors uncomplainingly. He wrote in his *Journal*:

I have been thoroughly wet with these rains more than once, yet without any harm at all. And I have lain many nights in the open air, and received all the dews that fell; and so, I believe, might any one, if his constitution was not impaired by the softness of a genteel education.

In the Georgia wilderness, with the rude huts of Savannah and Frederica housing financial failures, ne'er-do-wells, and ambitious scoundrels, as well as honest workingmen, Wesley decided to organize a Methodist Club after the Oxford fashion. In April, 1736, the companions agreed:

(1) to advise the more serious among them [the parishioners] to form themselves into a sort of little society, and to meet once or twice a week, in order to reprove, instruct, and exhort one another. (2) To select out of these a smaller number for a more intimate union with each other, which might be forwarded, partly by our conversing singly with each, and partly by inviting them all together to our house; and this, accordingly, we determined to do every Sunday in the afternoon.

At Savannah, John set about a house-to-house visitation of his parishioners, an evidence of zeal of which the trustees heard with approval the next year.

Even in this zealous ministry there was occasion for offense, since the High Churchmanship of the Wesleys was resented by their parishioners. John refused to baptize a child except by immersion unless the parents would signify that it was too weak for this method to be used with safety. In this he had the authority of church law, but he was acting contrary to common practice. "They say they are Protestants," one objector reported to Wesley, "but as for you, they cannot tell what religion you are of." John's chief entanglement, however, was in troubles in which Charles had become involved. Charles, serving as secretary to Oglethorpe, was at Frederica, where Oglethorpe was taken up with alarms of Spanish invasion. Charles's *Journal* is nervous with the continuous tension of the little English settlement expectant of Indian outrages and Spanish cruelties. In Frederica also were the two troublemakers, Mrs. Welch and Mrs. Hawkins, the surgeon's wife. These women confessed to Charles that they had been intimate with Oglethorpe. They then told Oglethorpe that the parson was circulating reports concerning them in Frederica. The purpose of the women in fomenting this trouble is hard to discern. Biographers of Wesley seem to think that they were both in love with Oglethorpe and designed breaking the puritanic influence which they imagined the Wesleys had over the Governor. The Wesleys later exonerated Oglethorpe of all blame, although they at first accepted the statement of the women at face value as accounting for the General's uncommon kindness to Mrs. Welch and Mrs. Hawkins on-board ship.

Whatever the truth of the charges against Oglethorpe, the result of the matter was that Charles was out of favor with his chief, who went so far as to leave him when attacked by fever without provisions or medical care. Charles, who was too proud to ask Oglethorpe for help, at last sent for his brother. John came at once, traveling the hundred miles from Savannah to Frederica for the first time. He was comforted on landing by turning to his Bible and finding as the first scripture on which his eye lighted—his favorite method of bibliomancy—the words, "If God be for us, who can be against us?" He at once helped his feeble brother to walk into the woods, where they discussed

49

the latter's affairs in Latin for fear of eavesdroppers. John remained six days and convinced Oglethorpe of his brother's innocence, but went away very doubtful of Oglethorpe. When, a few days later, news from the south made the General prepare to leave hurriedly with his men, he called for Charles. Someone had brought Oglethorpe his mourning sword by mistake, and the soldier was certain that he was going to his death. He and Charles had mutual explanations, and the General gave his secretary a ring with the assurance that this would procure him aid from powerful friends in England. "These letters," said Oglethorpe, "show that the Spaniards have long been seducing our allies, and intend to cut us off at a blow. I fall by my friends: Gascoigne [commander of the "Hawk"], whom I have made; the Carolina people, whom I depended upon to send their promised succours." Charles blessed him in Latin, the General quoted some of his own poetry, and the expedition set out.

Oglethorpe returned alive, and Charles was reinstated in the General's favor. For a few weeks Charles exchanged places with his brother, and John enjoyed the blessings of Frederica society. The reader might be spared the somewhat lurid pages in which John told of his trials at Frederica if they did not cast such a brilliant light upon conditions in the pioneer colony and upon the character of Wesley.

Charles had written at length to John concerning the situation at Frederica, taking care to hide in Greek his sentiments concerning Mrs. Welch and Mrs. Hawkins. When John arrived to take his brother's place, Mrs. Hawkins sent for him and inquired what was meant by two Greek words which had been used and which had been read by someone who pried into the correspondence. All the women in Frederica felt their honor involved, said Mrs. Hawkins. John gave a straightforward answer: that these were his brother's words used before the season of explanation which had ensued on the occasion of his previous visit; that no other women in town need be uneasy about them, for the words referred only to her and to Mrs. Welch. The logic of his answer was admirable, but the effect was unexpected by Wesley. She started up, called him a scoundrel, a pitiful rascal, and the like. Her husband came in, and she told him that John had said, "That dog [Charles] meant her by those d—d words." Hawkins joined in the chorus, and Wesley was grieved to tears. The trouble was carried to Oglethorpe, who rebuked the Hawkinses.

But the matter was not ended. A few days later Wesley was summoned again by Mrs. Hawkins. He went, but asked her maid to remain in the room. The amiable lady first drew a pistol and threatened to shoot him through the head with a brace of balls. When he seized that hand, she brandished a pair of scissors in the other. Then she threw herself on him and forced him back on the bed, crying that she would have his heart or his heart's blood. The scene cannot be told except in John's words. The Oxford fellow in the clutches of a termagant, was thinking first of the scandal.

I was very unwilling either to cry out, which must publish to all the world what, for her sake, I desired should be more private; or to attempt rising by force, which could not have been done without hurting her. Just then the maid came in, whom she ordered to reach a knife, swearing she would be the death of her if she did not. The woman stood trembling, not knowing what to do. Her two boys [servants] came in next, whom she bid to hold my hands, and I desired to take hold of their mistress. But they did not dare to do either. Then came in Mr. Davison the constable, and Mr. Reed, who, on my desire, were going to take her by the arms, when Mr. Hawkins came in, asked what that scoundrel did in his house, and commanded them at their peril not to touch his wife. Upon this encouragement she struggled again to get her hands loose; but not being able, seized on my cassock with her teeth and tore both the sleeves of it to pieces, and then fixed upon my arm, four men (for Mr. Robinson and Ward were now come) standing by, and not daring to hinder her. I then spoke to Mr. Hawkins, who, seeing the company increase, took her round the waist and lifted her up. I went to Mr. Oglethorpe and gave him a simple narration of what had happened. He sent for them both and for Mr. Horton. She defended all, saying he had not done her justice for the wrong she had received, and therefore she had done herself justice. After a long hearing, her husband and she, promising better behaviour for the future, were dismissed.

Charles had had enough of Georgia. Consequently at the first opportunity he resigned, and Oglethorpe accepted the resignation. The soldier offered a little advice to Charles on his departure:

On many accounts I should recommend to you marriage, rather than celibacy. You are of a social temper, and would find in a married state the difficulties of working out your salvation exceedingly lessened, and your helps as much increased.

Charles was intrusted with important documents for the trustees and embarked on the sixteenth of August for home. He had the bad fortune of a drunken captain and a leaking ship, so that after considerable delay in Boston, where they were landed for a time, he arrived a month overdue in London. There the ship had been given up for lost, to the intense distress of the trustees, who seemed not to be quite certain whether they were sorrowing for the supposedly shipwrecked parson or for the papers he carried with him.

John accompanied his brother to Charlestown and made some arrangements there for the publication of the hymnbook on which he was working—a book published in Charlestown the next year. Then he returned to take up his duties in Savannah. But he could not shake off his interest in Frederica. On the twelfth of October he consulted with his friends concerning the "poor people" of Frederica and decided that he should revisit them, leaving Ingham in charge at Savannah. The reader of the following pages will detect another reason for Wesley's concern with the Frederica parishioners.

In a colony with all too many coarse men and unscrupulous women, the young scholar had been attracted toward a girl of obvious innocence and still more obvious good looks. On March 13, 1736, Wesley had for the first time met Sophia Hopkey, niece of Causton, chief magistrate of Savannah. The young lady was about eighteen years old, attractive, intelligent, and possessed of some property in her own right. From the time of their first meeting, Sophia Hopkey appears at intervals in the diary. She and a friend were regular attendants, and sometimes the only ones, at Wesley's early-morning services. She was "open and affected," by which Wesley meant interested in religious matters. Gradually, "Miss Sophy" formed the habit of coming to the parsonage to discuss religious questions with the young clergyman. Early in their acquaintance she nursed him through an attack of fever. Miss Sophy's uncle, the magistrate Causton, soon saw the direction of his niece's affections and broadly hinted as much to Wesley.

When John returned from Charlestown, the young lady was at Frederica, sent there to get her away from a disreputable lover. When Wesley arrived at Frederica in October, 1736, he found Miss Sophy "scarce a shadow of what she was when [he] left her." He attributed her disconsolate appearance to the fact that supposedly "harmless company" had stolen away all her spiritual strength while he was gone and that most of her good resolutions were vanished. She told him that she was resolved to return to England. Her spiritual physician proceeded to prescribe for her. "I begged of her to pray earnestly to God to direct her to what was best. I then read to her some of the most affecting parts of the *Serious Call* and of Ephrem Syrus."

In the evening I asked Miss Sophy if she was still determined to go to England. On her answering "Yes," I offered several arguments drawn from the topics of religion against it. But they did not appear to make any impression. Then I pressed her upon the head of friendship. Upon which she burst into tears, and said, "Now my resolution begins to stagger"; as it did more and more every day.

When Wesley was ready to return to Savannah, it was determined by Oglethorpe that Miss Sophy should accompany him. The General, having advised Charles to marry, was determined himself to play cupid to John. The latter agreed to escort Miss Sophy, but wrote in his *Journal*:

I saw the danger to myself, but yet had a good hope I should be delivered out of it, (1) because it was not my choice which brought me into it; (2) because I still felt in myself the same desire and design to live a single life; and (3) because I was persuaded should my desire and design be changed, yet her resolution to live single would continue.

On the journey Wesley regaled his young charge with Bishop Patrick's *Prayers* and with the first volume of Fleury's *History of the Church*. Beginning "a close conversation" with her on the subject of "Christian holiness," he was delighted when she owned her ignorance and showed an earnest desire that he instruct her. Decidedly she was dear to him both as an object of love and as an audience. On the way to Savannah they spent one night on an island, crew and passengers sleeping around the campfire.

Observing in the night, the fire we lay by burning bright, that Miss Sophy was broad awake, I asked her, "Miss Sophy, how far are you engaged to Mr. Mellichamp [the worthless fellow to whom Miss Sophy was supposed to be engaged]?" She answered, "I have promised him either to marry him or to marry no one at all." I said (which indeed was the expression of a sudden wish, not of any formed design) "Miss Sophy, I should think myself happy if I was to spend my life with you." She burst out into tears and said, "I am every way unhappy. I won't have Tommy; for he is a bad man. And I can have none else." She added, "Sir, you don't know the danger you are in. I beg you would speak no word more on this head." And after a while, "When others have spoken to me on the subject, I felt an aversion to them. But I don't feel any to you. We may converse on other subjects as freely as ever." Both my judgment and will acquiesced in what she said, and we ended our conversation with a psalm.

Wesley continued to try to cure what he imagined to be Miss Sophy's religious ailment by liberal doses of the Greek Fathers and of later devotional writers. The idea of marriage he could not get out of his mind, but he could think up reasons against it, as " (1) because it would probably obstruct the design of my coming into America, the going among the Indians; and (2) because I was not strong enough to bear the complicated temptations of a married state."

Confident in his reasons, Wesley broadened the scope of his protégée's instructions. His daily program for her began to take sizable proportions.

Immediately after breakfast we all joined in Hickes's *Devotions.* She was then alone till eight. I taught her French between eight and nine, and at nine we joined in prayer again. She then read or wrote French till ten. In the evening I read to her and some others select parts of Ephrem Syrus, and afterwards Dean Young's and Mr. Reeve's *Sermons.* We always concluded with a psalm.

The role of impersonal tutor was hard to preserve, and the *Journal* testifies to his difficulties. "This I began with a single eye. But it was not long before I found it a task too hard for me to preserve the same intention with which I began, in such intimacy of conversation as ours was." The following quotation will show how hard his task really was:

Feb. 27, 1737. After all the company but Miss Sophy was gone, Mr. Delamotte went out and left us alone again. Finding her still the same, my resolution failed. At the end of a very serious conversation, I took her by the hand, and, perceiving she was not displeased, I was so utterly disarmed, that that hour I should have engaged myself for life, had it not been for the full persuasion of her entire sincerity, and in consequence of which I doubted not but she was resolved (as she had said) "never to marry while she lived."

A moment's reflection when she was gone convinced me that I had done foolishly. And I once more resolved by God's help to be more wary for the future. Accordingly, though I saw her every day in the following week, I touched her not.

Wesley consulted his Moravian friends and even cast lots to find out whether he should marry. The men he consulted were somewhat ambiguous; the lot said, "Think of it no more." He acquiesced cheerfully enough in so far that he made no further advances himself, but he showed some zeal in trying to dissuade the young lady from an engagement with another—her third lover. Miss Sophy gave the dilatory Wesley every opportunity to come back to the point; then, as he still delayed, she finally announced her engagement to one Williamson. At the end of a painful and fruitless interview with them both, Wesley exhorted the couple "to remember the many instructions and advices I had given her. I kissed them both," he concluded, "and took my leave of her as one I was to see no more."

I came home and went into my garden [continues the *Journal*]. I walked up and down, seeking rest but finding none. From the beginning of my life to this hour I had not known one such as this. God let loose my inordinate affection upon me, and the poison thereof drank up my spirit. I was as stupid as if half awake, and yet in the sharpest pain I ever felt. To see her no more: that thought was as the piercings of a sword; it was not to be borne, nor shaken off. I was weary of the world, of light, of life. Yet one way remained, to seek to God—a very present help in time of trouble. And I did seek after God, but I found Him not. I forsook Him before; now

He forsook me. I could not pray. Then indeed the snares of death were about me; the pains of hell overtook me. Yet I struggled for life; and though I had neither words nor thoughts, I lifted up my eyes to the Prince that is highly exalted, and supplied the place of them as I could: and about four o'clock He so far took the cup from me that I drank so deeply of it no more.

Before marrying, Miss Sophy waited a little longer, apparently hoping that Wesley would press his case. Then she ran off with Williamson and married him. Wesley immediately developed scruples about admitting her to Communion, on the ground that she had deceived him about the state of her heart concerning her lovers. At last he repelled her from the Communion on the technical charge that she had not given legal notification of her intention to communicate after an absence of several months. The husband responded with a suit for damages to the amount of one thousand pounds.

The affidavit which was filed accused Wesley of having attempted to seduce Sophia Hopkey, promising that she would be holier for living with him and that he would make his Methodistic requirements easier for her. This affidavit, a copy of which Wesley preserved with his papers, was sworn to by Sophia herself, August 16, 1737. The testimony against Wesley must be weighed with due regard to the character of his accusers. Causton, the magistrate, had been under suspicion and charges for several years. The trustees were constantly hearing complaints against him, and he was unquestionably overbearing, contentious, and very likely dishonest. Williamson was not remarkable for sense or religion according to Wesley, although something must be allowed here for bias. Nothing can be alleged against Sophia except that she was fascinated by the handsome young don, a Prince Charming from the world of which she had dreamed, and that to attract him she assumed a religious devotion which she did not feel. Her exasperation at his perverse restraint, coupled with natural resentment of his assumption of control over her, may well account for her willingness to ruin him.

In support of Wesley's account of his conduct should be quoted the opinions of two competent witnesses who were in position to know the facts. The Rev. Alexander Gordon, commissary of the church in Carolina, wrote the Bishop of London that "however he [Wesley] might not be acquitted of some imprudence and unguarded conversation, yet he verily believed him innocent of anything criminal either in fact or intention." Lord Egmont, as will appear later, with all the evidence before him thought Wesley had been indiscreet, but in no way criminal. That Wesley was in love with Sophia is beyond doubt, but the conflict of his desires and his own scruples accounts for his strange conduct. He repelled Miss Sophy from the Communion and then rationalized his motives for doing so. There was also a domineering attitude on his part that Williamson and Miss Sophy alike had cause to resent. The record will exonerate Wesley from the gross charges brought against him; it will not bear witness to his having used good sense or even ordinary tact.

The grand jury indicted Wesley on ten counts, nine of them relating to ecclesiastical usages, as his refusal to baptize a child by other than immersion unless the parents would testify that the child was too weak for such baptism, and his refusal to read the burial service over the body of a dissenter. The tenth count was on the complaint of Sophia. A minority dissented from this presentment, but Causton had used all his influence to procure a return against Wesley. In doing so the magistrate rendered himself so obnoxious to the grand jury that they returned against him at the same sitting, and a year later he was removed from office on a charge of embezzlement.

Wesley appeared to answer the charges but refused to plead on the nine ecclesiastical points, alleging that the court had no jurisdiction in such matters. In this he was technically right, although the charges were mainly sustainable. Wesley's High

Church practices were well known and extremely offensive to many of his parishioners. But they were also legal. Alexander Gordon said that the ecclesiastical charges were "all either impertinent, false, or frivolous"; and Lord Egmont upon inquiry found to his astonishment that Wesley was acting within his rights in his High Church requirements. On the tenth point, Sophia Williamson's charges, Wesley asked for immediate trial.

While he waited for the trial which never took place, he went about his duties and summed up his observations concerning the colony and its surroundings. Charles had already given Lord Egmont an account of the state of the colony which spoke well for the Wesleys' powers of observation. John now recorded in his *Journal* a short, but very careful, survey of Georgia.

The Indians, whom once he had pictured as "noble savages" living the "life of Nature," he had learned were far from the idyllic creatures of eighteenth-century imaginings. He speaks best of the Georgia Indians, but his account of them is not flattering:

Every one doeth what is right in his own eyes; and if it appears wrong to his neighbour, the person aggrieved usually steals on the other unawares, and shoots him, scalps him, or cuts off his ears. . . . They are likewise all, except perhaps the Choctaws, gluttons, drunkards, thieves, dissemblers, liars. They are implacable, unmerciful; murderers of fathers, murderers of mothers, murderers of their own children—it being a common thing for a son to shoot his father or mother because they are old and past labour, and for a woman either to procure abortion, or to throw her child into the next river, because she will go with her husband to the war.

This was the account of the Indians which passed for true among colonists living in fear of attack, and there was plenty of evidence to support such an account. A Frenchman from New Orleans had told Wesley of his capture by savages.

I and one more were saved by the warrior who took us [ran the Frenchman's story]. The manner of burning the rest was holding lighted canes to their arms and legs, and several parts of their bodies, for some time, and then for a while taking them away. They likewise stuck burning pieces of wood into their flesh all round, in which condition they kept them from morning till evening.

As to the Indians' daily life, the Frenchman said that "they do nothing but eat and drink, and smoke, from morning till night; and, in a manner, from night till morning." "See the religion of Nature truly delineated!" exclaimed Wesley.

Next to the Indians, Wesley had been interested in the German emigrants. They were from a colony of Bohemian refugees who had been given shelter on the Saxon estates of a German pietist, Count Zinzendorf. One of the picturesque figures of the eighteenth century, Zinzendorf had organized a community of these Moravians; and from this settlement at Herrnhut, in Saxony, missionaries had been sent to Greenland, the West Indies, South America, and Africa. Wesley had been first attracted to these Moravians when on shipboard they had been unafraid during the storms. He had talked with their leaders and observed the life of the emigrants. He admired their systematic, simple method of living and their apparent peace and joy. Their teaching was that man is saved by faith, an inner trust, rather than by laborious obedience or performance of good works. All through his stay in Georgia, Wesley had gone to them for advice; and he devoted his time in his last hurried days, when he was expecting the grand jury's action, to a careful chronicle of a theological conversation with one of their leaders.

Wesley's interest in Georgia was now exhausted. He saw no possibility of instructing the Indians, nor in spite of Tomochachi's welcoming address, had he heard "of any Indians on the Continent of America who had the least desire of being instructed." He felt under no obligations to Savannah except to tell the trustees the true state of the colony. Since the magistrates would not set the date for his trial, he posted a notice that he intended leaving and prepared to depart. The magistrates published an order forbidding his going, but made no effort to detain him. His leaving was the easiest solution of the matter for them. Accordingly, the evening of December 2, 1737, John Wesley left Savannah for Charlestown, where he set sail for England.

A disappointed and disillusioned man, having seen a kind of life of which he had never dreamed, having learned how little he could depend upon his fellows or upon himself, Wesley came away haunted by the assurance and peace of the simple German peasants whom neither outward storms nor inward passions seemed to disturb. "I went to America, to convert the Indians," he wrote on his homeward voyage, "but oh, who shall convert me?"

CHAPTER IV

Pilgrim's Progress

On FEBRUARY 1, 1738, John Wesley landed at Deal, missing Whitefield, who was leaving for America, by only a day. Charles was surprised with the news of his brother's arrival, but understood that he had returned to tell the true state of the colony of Georgia. Oglethorpe, who was in England at the time, was uneasy at the news and thought that Wesley should not have come back without leave of the trustees.

On the eighth Wesley waited on the trustees and gave them "a short but plain account of the state of the colony." He told them that about one hundred idle persons in Georgia had left within two months. The year before, the people had been able to supply corn enough for only half the colony; and half the trees in the garden were dead. He added that the colony was healthy and gave a good report of the industry of the Salzburgers. The trustees seemed surprised at Wesley's account of the fewness of the people, and Oglethorpe told Charles that there was a strong spirit rising against John, because people said that he had come back to do mischief to the colony.

Georgia affairs were in a critical condition. The trustees were trying to obtain more support, but they were meeting strong opposition which threatened the very existence of the colony. There were bitter disputes with Carolina, and to add to their troubles, there were rumors that Oglethorpe would be displaced for fear that he might embroil the nation with Spain. It was at this juncture that Wesley returned with his report of bad conditions.

On February 22 Wesley appeared again before the trustees and gave them several papers and certificates for his own justification, "whereby," concluded Egmont in his diary, "it appeared indeed that he was guilty of indiscretion, but that Causton our head bailiff was much more to blame." So serious were the charges which Wesley made against Causton that Lord Egmont attributed to them the resignation of two of the council. "In truth," observed Egmont, "the bad account of Causton's behaviour brought over by Mr. Wesley, our minister at Savannah, is enough to make all of us quit."

As to the charges against Wesley, the trustees seem to have been satisfied that they amounted to little beside proof of errors of judgment. Causton's previous record would discount his testimony, and the trustees were disposed to accept Wesley's new accusations against the head bailiff of Savannah. But when, on Wednesday, April 26, Wesley left his license as minister of Savannah with the trustees, thus resigning his work there, they accepted it "with great pleasure," for he appeared to them "to be a very odd mixture of a man, an enthusiast and at the same time a hypocrite, wholly distasteful to the greater part of the inhabitants, and an incendiary of the people against the magistracy."

Thus Wesley returned to England to be cleared of the charges against him, but to have his resignation accepted with great pleasure. His Oxford experiences had inured him to others' disapproval, but now he was himself convinced that his mission to America had been largely a failure. With his rigorous, even ascetic views he could not but look upon his passion for Sophia Hopkey as a victory of his lower nature. The sojourn in America, so he wrote in his *Journal,* had "in some measure" humbled him and shown him what was in his heart. He had learned also that his judgment of men was very fallible. Charles once said of his brother that he "was born for the benefit of knaves." Reflecting on his experiences in the colony, John Wesley remarked that they had taught him "to 'beware of men.' "

There had been some gains from the Georgia experience, according to his judgment; and they were chiefly four. He had learned to read German, Spanish, and Italian—he already knew French. He had been confirmed in his belief that he could leave his affairs to be directed of the Lord, using the lot where he had no other means of discerning the divine will. He had been delivered from his fear of the sea, a heritage of his childhood in Lincolnshire. Finally, he had come to know the Moravians, whom he considered model Christians.

Looking over this characteristic summary of personal losses and gains in Georgia, one can understand the way which Wesley was going. His search for Christian perfection through self-discipline, by good works, by a strict adherence to what he believed to be the practice of the Primitive Church, his discouragement as the result of his experiences in the New World, all prepared Wesley for a rearrangement of his life pattern. He was ready for a mystical conversion of the type experienced by Luther and Paul—although not of the type recorded by Augustine. Taught by the Moravians to believe that a personal attitude ("faith") is sufficient for salvation, and that one can accept his salvation as an accomplished fact, not as something to be striven after, Wesley was consciously seeking just such a rearrangement of his inner life as came to him. Psychologically he was ready to enter upon a time when confidence would supplant his previous fear, when all the energy which had been taken up in inner conflicts would be released into the one channel which with few exceptions was to be the sole outlet of his energies to the end of his days—the propagation of what he called practical religion. The familiar account of Wesley's conversion experience may be quoted again. The day was Wednesday, May 24, 1738.

I think it was about five this morning, that I opened my Testament on those words, . . . "There are given unto us exceeding great and precious promises, even that ye should be partakers of the divine nature.". . . Just as I went out, I opened it again on those words, "Thou art not far from the kingdom of God." In the afternoon I was asked to go to St. Paul's. The anthem was, "Out of the deep have I called unto Thee, O Lord: Lord, hear my voice. O let Thine ears consider well the voice of my complaint. If Thou, Lord, wilt be extreme to mark what is done amiss, O Lord, who may abide it? For there is mercy with Thee; therefore shalt Thou be feared. O Israel, trust in the Lord: for with the Lord there is mercy, and with Him is plenteous redemption. And He shall redeem Israel from all his sins."

In the evening I went very unwillingly to a society in Aldersgate Street, where one was reading Luther's preface to the *Epistle to the Romans*. About a quarter before nine, while he was describing the change which God works in the heart through faith in Christ, I felt my heart strangely warmed. I felt I did trust in Christ, Christ alone for salvation; and an assurance was given me that He had taken away *my* sins, even *mine,* and saved *me* from the law of sin and death.

With the zeal of a new convert Wesley set about persuading others that they must have just such an experience as he himself had had. Charles had been converted a few days before and was a willing ally in the new proselyting efforts of his brother. In later years John was to change his mind as to the necessity of everyone undergoing just such an inner adjustment as had been his lot, but at this time he had no doubts, and his zeal was disturbing to less enthusiastic souls. The mother of James Hutton, a bookseller "at the Bible and Sun without Temple Bar," became so alarmed that she wrote Samuel Wesley at Tiverton:

Your brother John seems to be turned a wild enthusiast, or fanatic, and, to our very great affliction, is drawing our two children into these wild notions by their great opinion of Mr. John's sanctity and judgment. It would be a great charity to many other honest well-meaning, simple souls, as well as to my children, if you could either confine or convert Mr. John when he is with you. For after his behaviour on Sunday, May 28, when you hear it, you will think him a not quite right man. Without even acquainting Mr. Hutton with any of his notions or designs, when Mr. Hutton had ended a sermon of Bishop Blackall's, which he had been reading in his study to a great number of people; Mr. John got up and told the people that five days before he was not a Christian, and this he was as well assured of as that five days before he was not in that room, and the way for them all to be Christians was to believe, and own that they were not now Christians.

Mrs. Hutton concluded with some wild stories about a ball of fire reported to have fallen upon a young woman and to have "fired her soul," and of a young man who dreamed of meeting God and Christ.

Samuel was bothered, but he seemed more interested in hearing details than in taking practical steps to confine or convert John. He would like to know about the ball of fire—"an odd sort of fire that"—and what that had to do with his brothers. Mrs. Hutton, good woman, had been vague as to the connection. The stories, if they were connected with his brothers, looked like signs of madness. "I do not hold it at all unlikely that perpetual intenseness of thought, and want of sleep, may have disordered my brother. I have been told that the Quaker's introversion of thought has ended in madness." And of this last he added, with a curious anticipation of modern psychology, "It is a studious stopping of every thought as fast as it arises, in order to receive the spirit." He concluded with a pious prayer that God would "stop the progress of this lunacy."

John, far from being stopped, was now all aflame with the ambition to visit Herrnhut, in Saxony, the home of the Moravians. He had embarked for Georgia hoping to learn the true gospel by studying the reactions of the "noble savage" to his preaching; disappointed there, he now believed that Herrnhut would prove his spiritual El Dorado. He had now, he thought, learned the first lesson of the gospel; he hoped that "conversing with those holy men who were themselves living witnesses of the full power of faith, and yet able to bear with those that are weak" would be a means of "establishing" his soul. He plunged at once into plans for this new pilgrimage and on the twelfth of June left for Germany.

The company included five Englishmen and three Germans. Beside Benjamin Ingham, Wesley took along a tailor by the name of Viney, who spoke German, for Wesley's German acquired from the Moravians was as yet imperfect. Along the way the little party was entertained by kindred spirits, for they found groups of pietists in nearly every city. Wesley's *Journal* is as usual filled with a mixture of comments upon strange scenery and religious conditions.

In Holland the pilgrims were astonished at a new treatment "which is not heard of in England." Several inns refused to entertain them, and Wesley remarks coldly on both the hospitality which he finally obtained and the sights of the towns. But Amsterdam roused his enthusiasm:

> The exact neatness of all the buildings here, the nice cleanness of the streets (which, we were informed, were all washed twice a week), and the canals which run through all the main streets, with rows of trees on either side, make this the pleasantest city which I have ever seen.

Cologne received scant praise from the now somewhat weary pedestrians. It was "the ugliest, dirtiest city I ever yet saw with my eyes," said Wesley. The cathedral was "mere heaps upon heaps: a huge, misshapen thing, which has no more of symmetry than of neatness belonging to it." He added some details in a letter to his mother: "Many of the stones broken, the windows dusty and full of cobwebs, and the pavement less clean than that of many English stables."

Wesley shared prevailing sentiment concerning Gothic, preferring Wren's work to the great cathedrals of his own land; but in justification of his criticism of Cologne one should remember that the cathedral was unfinished in 1738 and was doubtless as misshapen as Wesley says. Besides, the neat soul of the little scholar revolted at the dirty German buildings and yearned for the nice cleanness of Dutch streets which were washed twice a week.

The views from his Rhine boat were described by Wesley in a letter to his mother. In his *Journal* he merely made the conventional eighteenth-century comment that the castles on the crags afforded some "agreeable prospects." But Wesley's mind was excited by his approach to Marienborn, where he was to meet the great Count Zinzendorf, head of the Moravian Church. Here he filled his *Journal* with theological notes gained from conversations, chiefly in Latin, with his hosts.

The Moravians later related several incidents which they said happened at Marienborn, but which Wesley did not record. They said that Wesley was not allowed to receive the Communion, because he was thought to be *homo perturbatus*—whatever they meant by that. Wesley, according to the Moravian account, was offended by this, but concealed his displeasure at the time. A story was also circulated to the effect that the Count, seeing how prim the Englishman was, once took him straight from working in the garden to call upon a distinguished family without giving him time to change his clothes. Whatever may have been Wesley's later conclusions upon these incidents—if, indeed, they really happened—at the time he was too much entranced by the apparent happiness of the Moravian settlement to feel other than kindly toward the Germans.

After two weeks with the Count, Wesley continued on his

journey to Herrnhut. At Weimar the friends were detained for some time at the gate and finally taken before "I know not what great man (I believe the Duke) ." The duke inquired where they were going and why; to which Wesley answered that they were going to Herrnhut, "to see the place where the Christians live." The duke looked hard and let them go. At Jena, Wesley noted the swords which the students carried and wondered at the new mileposts which the elector had set up in his territory. At the gates of Halle they had experience of the King of Prussia's famous guard of tall men. By them the friends were sent about from gate to gate until Wesley sent in a note to Professor Francke, son of one of the most famous of German pietists, August Hermann Francke. Francke was not then in the city, but the letter admitted them, and the travelers inspected the Orphan House, one of Francke's outstanding charities.

At Meissen, Wesley was interested in the chinaware made there. He thought it was as finely shaped and colored as any he had ever seen. At church he was astonished at the costliness and gaudiness of the people's clothing. The women wore huge fur caps of the shape of a Turkish turban, with one or more ribands hanging down a great length behind. The minister was adorned with gold and scarlet with a great cross both behind and before. Most of the men kept their hats on, even during prayers; and very few received the Sacrament. The scandalized Englishman could only exclaim, "Alas, alas! what a *Reformed* country is this!"

At Dresden the little company was carried from one magistrate to another for two hours before they were allowed to go to their inn. Wesley's indignation explodes in his *Journal:*

I greatly wonder that common sense and common humanity (for these doubtless subsist in Germany as well as England) do not put an end to this senseless, inhuman usage of strangers which we met with at almost every German city, though more particularly at

Frankfort, Weimar, Halle, Leipzig, and Dresden. I know nothing that can reasonably be said in its defence in a time of full peace, being a breach of all the common, even heathen laws of hospitality.

On the first of August, Wesley came at last to Herrnhut, about thirty miles from Dresden. Here he remained for eleven days, observing the customs and inquiring into the history and doctrines of the Moravians. His *Journal* gives short biographies of Christian David and other well-known characters of the Moravian community, and a copy of the constitution of the church. The information is given with few comments, but presents a well-rounded picture of the unusual settlement, which under Zinzendorf's leadership had become the center of the most intense missionary activities of the eighteenth century. The Moravians later claimed that, since Wesley understood German imperfectly, he had mistaken many things about Moravian doctrine and life. The material in the *Journal,* however, gives the impression that on the whole Wesley gained a tolerably accurate conception of the community.

On the twelfth of August he set out on the long journey home. At Halle he found Professor Francke at home, "who behaved with the utmost humanity." At Jena, Wesley visited the schools for poor children and inquired into their history and methods. Johann Franz Buddeus (1667-1729), whose scientific compendium was later used by Wesley, had been one of the founders of these schools.

The first evening out from Cologne, Wesley met a company of "Switzers" rejoicing on their way to Georgia. He considered them given into his hands by God and "plainly told them what manner of place it was." Having thus delivered his soul, he hastened through Holland and on September 16 reached London.

Sometime within the next two weeks Wesley wrote to the church at Herrnhut, frankly expressing his mind concerning them. For some reason the letter was never sent, and this was just as well, since it was hardly the kind that is sent to one's hosts immediately after a visit. Wesley had been pleased with many things which he saw, so ran the letter, but he had some doubts and would mention them "in love and meekness." These doubts were set out in sixteen questions, whose burden can be gathered from these examples:

Is not the Count all in all? Are not the rest mere shadows, calling him Rabbi, almost implicitly both believing and obeying him? . . . Are you in general serious enough? . . . Do you not magnify your own Church too much? . . . Do you not use cunning, guile, or dissimulation in many cases?

The letter shows that Wesley had been once more disappointed in his search for a community perfectly expressing his ideal of Christianity. Just as America had disillusioned him as to the myth of the "noble savage," so Germany dispelled his hopes of finding in the Moravians the Utopian church. He was being slowly driven toward launching a movement of his own which should propagate the faith as he understood it.

On his return Wesley began preaching, uniting with a society of persons of like mind which had been organized recently from members of the Church of England. His *Journal* for September 17 reads:

I began again to declare in my own country the glad tidings of salvation, preaching three times, and afterwards expounding the Holy Scripture to a large company in the Minories. On *Monday* I rejoiced to meet with our little society, which now consisted of thirty-two persons. The next day I went to the condemned felons in Newgate, and offered them free salvation. In the evening I went to a society in Bear Yard, and preached repentance and remission of sins. The next evening I spoke the truth in love at a society in Aldersgate Street.

71

The following weeks were occupied with preaching at various churches in London and with a journey to Oxford on which he read over with great interest the account of the revival in New England under the leadership of Jonathan Edwards. At Oxford he had a remarkable experience which crowds theology off the pages of his *Journal*.

On *Monday* night [runs his entry for November 19] I was greatly troubled in dreams; and about eleven o'clock waked in an unaccountable consternation, without being able to sleep again. About that time (as I found in the morning) one who had been designed to be my pupil, but was not, came into the Porter's lodge (where several persons were sitting) with a pistol in his hand. He presented this, as in sport, first at one and then at another. He then attempted twice or thrice to shoot himself, but it would not go off. Upon his laying it down one took it up, and blew out the priming. He was very angry, went and got fresh prime, came in again, sat down, beat the flint with his key, and about twelve, pulling off his hat and wig, said he would die like a gentleman, and shot himself through the head.

There was some discussion of Charles returning to residence at Oxford. Charles demurred at this, but there were no settled plans for either brother as yet. They were preaching wherever they had opportunity, but opportunities were rapidly diminishing; for by the end of 1738 most London churches had closed against them because of their enthusiastic preaching of the doctrine of mystical conversion. This preaching shocked not only easygoing churchmen but also many earnest men incapable by temperament or training of mystical experiences.

Very soon after his return from Germany, John accompanied Charles in a call upon the Bishop of London, Edmund Gibson, the greatest church lawyer in England. They discussed first whether those who had been baptized by dissenters should be required to be rebaptized before admission into the Church of England, and on this subject the Whig bishop took a more liberal view than the Methodists. The brothers then pressed him to decide whether religious societies were illegal. The shrewd bishop refused to commit himself, advising them to read the Acts for themselves, but promising to receive no accusation against them unless presented by two or three witnesses, as the law required.

While Wesley was in London, meeting with such religious societies as were hospitable and uncertain as to his next step, he was suddenly confronted with an invitation to take part in an irregular, but highly promising religious enterprise begun by the meteoric Whitefield. The latter had returned in December, 1738, intent upon being ordained for further service in America and upon taking collections for various projects he had in mind for the colonies. When he had left England a year before, just as John Wesley returned, he had been the most popular preacher in London; but he returned to find his reputation much damaged. In his absence his voyage journals had been printed and had aroused unfavorable comment, for Whitefield was given to loose expressions signifying that he had been specially favored of the Almighty. Upon his return, therefore, Whitefield began preaching in the face of criticism; and the opposition came to a climax when there was a misunderstanding about an invitation to preach in St. Margaret's, Westminster, and the newspapers unfairly reported the incident as a disgraceful brawl. Whitefield departed shortly after this for the west of England.

At Bath, Whitefield asked for the use of the abbey and was refused. At Bristol the rector of St. Mary's, Redcliffe, also declined to open his pulpit to the young minister of Savannah. Shut out from the churches, Whitefield began to preach at the jail by favor of the keeper, Dagge, later immortalized by Dr. Johnson for humane treatment of the poet Savage. Not content with this, the evangelist began speaking in the fields to the miners of Kingswood. Thus, almost accidentally, began the field preaching which was to characterize the Methodists for a half century.

Whitefield continued until he felt that he must return to America, and on March 22 he wrote Wesley to come to Bristol and continue the work there. The seriousness with which Wesley took this proposal is hard to understand at this distance. The modern reader cannot appreciate the feeling of abhorrence with which the eighteenth century looked upon so innocent a proceeding as preaching in the fields. But for Wesley to go to Bristol and identify himself with Whitefield's erratic methods was something which he could not do without evidence of divine approval. His *Journal* entries show the way in which at this time he went about determining the sentiments of the Deity.

The first method was that of opening the Bible and taking as an expression of the will of God either the verse at the top of the page or the one on which the eye fell. The results of the first trials were discouraging enough. "Get thee up into this mountain . . . ," read the first, "and die in the mount whither thou goest up, and be gathered unto thy people." The others were not much better: "And the children of Israel wept for Moses in the plains of Moab thirty days." "I will shew him how great things he must suffer for my name's sake." "And devout men carried Stephen to his burial, and made great lamentation over him."

Since the oracles were unpropitious, the religious society in Fetter Lane was consulted. They could come to no decision and resorted to lot. The lot was favorable to his departure. Having learned this much, some were curious to know how the adventure would result; resorting to scripture, they obtained the following cryptic verses:

Now there was long war between the house of Saul and the house of David: but David waxed stronger and stronger, and the house of Saul waxed weaker and weaker. . . . When wicked men have slain a righteous person in his own house upon his bed? shall I not . . . require his blood of your hand, and take you away from the earth? . . . And Ahaz slept with his fathers, and was buried with his fathers in the city of David.

The one whom these oracles most concerned seems not to have questioned who was David and who was Saul or who was the righteous man slain upon his bed, but, leaving Ahaz sleeping with his fathers, on March 29, 1739, Wesley set out for Bristol.

CHAPTER V

The Lord's Cavalry

B̲ristol, to which John Wesley came in the spring of 1739, was, as Daniel Defoe had said, "the greatest, the richest, and the best Point of Trade in Great Britain, London only excepted." This importance was due in the main to trade with America and the West Indies, a trade which determined largely the character of the city. Seafaring men returning from long cruises did not add to the moral tone of the community; a few years later Bristol was said to have had alehouses in the proportion of one to each ten houses in the city. Slave ships sailed regularly from the harbor, and many privateers were outfitted there. Near the city was the mining community of Kingswood, where Whitefield had begun preaching in the fields.

On the evening of March 31 Wesley arrived in Bristol and met Whitefield.

I could scarce reconcile myself [wrote Wesley] to this strange way of preaching in the fields, of which he set me an example on Sunday; having been all my life (till very lately) so tenacious of every point relating to decency and order, that I should have thought the saving of souls almost a sin if it had not been done in a church.

The eighteenth century had a hard struggle to overcome its repugnance to unadorned nature. In the middle of the century men saw nothing "romantic" in the spectacle of a clergyman performing his duties with the sky for his canopy and a mound for his pulpit. A man who, like Wesley, loved the decency and order of Anglican worship and preferred what was "neat" and "nice" instinctively turned away also from the noisy mobs which attended preaching in the fields. But Whitefield's example prevailed.

On Monday, April 2, 1739, Wesley took the decisive step which freed him from dependence upon favors of the clergy— bishops and priests alike. "At four in the afternoon," runs the record of that day, "I submitted to be more vile, and proclaimed in the highways the glad tidings of salvation, speaking from a little eminence in a ground adjoining to the city, to about three thousand people."

The preaching of Wesley and his friends, which was to raise such a furor in England, merits some description. Whitefield, the innovator in the matter of field preaching, was at this time twenty-five years old. He had begun to lose the graceful figure of youth and was assuming that corpulency which is so evident in his pictures. He had a squint in one eye, the effect of measles, which earned him the title "Dr. Squintum." In preaching he was emotional and dramatic. Lecky has given a classic description of Whitefield as a preacher.

His preaching [wrote the historian] combined almost the highest perfection of acting with the most burning fervour of conviction. No man ever exhibited more wonderfully the strange power which great histrionic talent exercises over the human mind—investing words which are in truth the emptiest bombast with all the glow of the most majestic eloquence, and imparting, for the moment at least, to confident assertions more than the weight of the most convincing arguments. His gestures were faultless in their beauty and propriety, while his voice was so powerful that Franklin, who was the most accurate of men, ascertained by experiment that it could be heard distinctly in the open air by 30,000 persons. . . . Garrick is reported to have said, with a pardonable exaggeration, that Whitefield could pronounce the word Mesopotamia in such a way as to move an audience to tears.

77

Garrick was much impressed with Whitefield's histrionic ability. "I would give a hundred guineas," he is said to have remarked, "if I could only say 'Oh!' like Mr. Whitefield." Dr. Johnson thought that Whitefield substituted "familiarity and noise" for "knowledge, art, and elegance"; but popular opinion did not agree with the Oracle. Benjamin Franklin, who printed some of Whitefield's works, has a well-known passage attesting the evangelist's powers of persuasion. The Philadelphian had no interest in an orphan house in Georgia and advised Whitefield to move it to Pennsylvania. When Whitefield refused, Franklin declined to contribute. A little while after, Franklin went to hear the preacher.

I silently resolved [said Franklin] he should get nothing from me. I had in my pocket a handful of copper money, three or four silver dollars, and five pistoles in gold. As he proceeded I began to soften, and concluded to give the copper. Another stroke of his oratory determined me to give the silver; and he finished so admirably that I emptied my pocket into the collection dish, gold and all. At this sermon there was also one of our Club, who, being of my sentiments respecting the building in Georgia, and suspecting a collection might be intended, emptied his pocket before he came from home. Toward the conclusion of the discourse, however, he felt a strong inclination to give, and applied to a neighbor who stood near him, to lend him money for the purpose. The request was fortunately made to, perhaps, the only man in the company who had the firmness not to be affected by the preacher. His answer was, "At any other time, friend Hopkinson, I would lend thee freely, but not now, for thee seems to be out of thy right senses."

Even the fastidious Chesterfield could be moved by the impassioned preaching of the evangelist. Once, listening to Whitefield's description of a blind beggar tottering on the edge of a precipice, the arbiter of fashion, forgetting where he was, cried out, "Good God! He's gone!"

Such lively testimony may now be supplemented by the ob-

servations of a methodical and able mind disposed to fair judgments. Lord Egmont heard Whitefield preach on June 8, 1739,
before his departure for America. Egmont sat in his summer
house with some guests invited "to partake of the curiosity" and
listened to Whitefield preaching to about two hundred people
assembled on the common.

The multitude, about 200, being assembled, he began with the
hundredth psalm, which numbers joined in. Then he made a long
pathetic prayer, and lastly, began his sermon with a clear and
audible voice. The subject of it was the necessity of the being born
again, or the new birth, which he said our present divines neglect
to teach, and even oppose from arguments of human reason, looking
upon those who hold it, and on himself in particular, as a madman,
an enthusiast and the like, whereas it is the doctrine of the Church
of England expressed in her thirty-nine articles, prayers and collects,
and literally asserted in the Holy Scriptures. . . . That by the sin of
Adam we were all under sin, and must have been damned but for
the free and gracious sufferings of Jesus Christ; but though this be
our condition, yet everybody that pleases may obtain this free grace
by praying for it. It is therefore by faith in Christ alone that we are
saved, not by our works, for being dead in sin we could do none;
but without good works we may assure ourselves that we have not
that faith; for they necessarily go together. He pressed the belief of
the Holy Trinity, and in the course of his sermon showed himself
a firm Church of England man. He preached by heart with much
earnestness, and spreading his arms wide, and was at no loss for
matter of words, and the people were very attentive.

This pedestrian account is supplemented by two pages of
impressions gained from extended questioning of the preacher
after the sermon. The diarist summed up his impressions with
this pronouncement:

This is the main of my conversation with him, by which I only
find an enthusiastic notion of his being capable of doing much
good, and perhaps he thinks he is raised up for that purpose; for
the rest, I believe him perfectly sincere and disinterested, and that

he does indeed work a considerable reformation among the common people, and there is nothing in his doctrine that can be laid hold on to his hurt.

There was the greatest contrast between the preaching of Whitefield and that of Wesley. John Hampson, who had been closely associated with Wesley, compared his style to "the calm, equal flow of a placid stream, gliding gently within its banks, without the least ruffle or agitation upon its surface," while Whitefield "alternately thundered and lightened upon his audience." The same hand wrote a discriminating criticism of Wesley as a preacher:

His attitude in the pulpit was graceful and easy; his action calm and natural, yet pleasing and expressive; his voice not loud, but clear and manly; his style neat, simple, perspicuous: and admirably adapted to the capacity of his hearers.

His discourses, in point of composition, were extremely different, on different occasions. When he gave himself sufficient time for study, he succeeded; and when he did not, he frequently failed. A clear proof, that the employments, in which he was engaged, were too numerous, and the economy, to which he gave himself up, too tedious and minute, for a man who generally appeared in the pulpit twice or thrice a-day. We have frequently heard him, when he was excellent, acute and ingenious in his observations, accurate in his descriptions, and clear and pointed in his expositions. Not seldom however have we found him the reverse. . . . Many have remarked, that when he fell into anecdote and story-telling, which was not seldom, his discourses were little to the purpose. The remark is true. We have scarcely ever heard from him a tolerable sermon, in which a story was introduced.

Wesley was not incapable of emotion in his preaching, and his quiet manner was often enlivened. Horace Walpole once heard him, thought him as "manifest an actor" as Garrick, and deplored the fact that "toward the end, he exalted his voice, and acted very ugly enthusiasm." Wesley's voice, while not capable of the tonal effects which were a part of Whitefield's stock in trade, was nevertheless noted for its carrying quality. By actual test it was found that he could be heard 140 yards.

The strength of Wesley's preaching seems to have been in the simplicity of his message, which was delivered with piercing directness. As a young preacher he had noticed that his congregation did not understand his sermons, and he asked an intelligent serving maid to hear him read a sermon and to stop him at every word she did not understand. Her "stop, sir" came annoyingly often; but every time Wesley resolutely substituted an easy word for a hard one. His models of style were the epistles of John. When John Nelson, later a Methodist preacher, heard Wesley for the first time, he thought that the preacher spoke to none but him and durst not look up, thinking that all the people were looking at him. Martin Madan, cousin of the poet Cowper and a man of fortune, was a member of the Hell Fire Club, a company of reckless spirits who urged Madan to hear Wesley and imitate his preaching for their entertainment. Madan went to Wesley's chapel, and as he entered the door, Wesley announced his text, "Prepare to meet thy God." The roisterer heard the sermon and returned to his companions. When asked if he had "taken off" the preacher, he answered quietly that the preacher "had taken him off." A little while afterward Madan became an evangelical preacher.

In his preaching Wesley knew how to turn circumstances to his advantage. Once in a Welsh churchyard a passing bell was tolling as he spoke, and he took up the words, "It is appointed unto men once to die." At Kingswood he preached under a sycamore tree during a violent rainstorm. His text was: "As the rain cometh down . . . from heaven, and returneth not thither, but watereth the earth, and maketh it bring forth and bud, . . . so shall my word be that goeth forth out of my mouth."

The spectacle of a clergyman in full canonicals preaching from a table in the street or from a mound on the common was so unusual in eighteenth-century England as to attract a crowd anywhere. To hear there or in the improvised meetinghouses which were rented or built during the first years of the movement language which could be understood by miners and drudges was equally as rare a thing. There were many learned and pious men in the priesthood of the Church of England, but most of them were content to fight infidelity in ponderous volumes which demolished their opponent's arguments, but were never read. The reader of eighteenth-century sermons or theological works does not wonder that the Wesleys and Whitefield had crowds to hear them wherever they went.

Preaching alone does not explain the Methodist meetings; the singing there was of a kind unheard before in England. Until 1737 there was no hymnbook intended for use in Church of England services.[1] Psalms were drawled out in the congregation, the tune set by a clerk whose sniveling voice often neutralized such little effect as feeble metrical versions might have had. The new Methodist movement was a singing movement. Charles Wesley in the course of his life wrote some six thousand hymns. If they were not all poetry, they were singable. Such rhymes as the following set miners and drudges singing in spite of themselves:

> O Jesus the Rest
> Of Spirits distrest,
> Receive a Lost Sinner that flies to thy Breast!
> Long tost on a Sea
> Of Trouble, I flee
> To find an Asylum, and Pardon in Thee.

If many of the songs were pure doggerel, others, such as "Love divine, all loves excelling" and "Jesus, Lover of my

[1] In this year John Wesley published his Charlestown hymnbook. Ten years before, a collection of hymns had been published by a churchman, but with the statement that they were not designed for use in the church services.

soul," have been sung all over the world. But the people who came to Methodist meetings were not literary critics; they wanted words they could sing to lively tunes, and lively ones they had. Sober churchmen heard with horror the tunes written by Charles Wesley, who did not scruple even to set words to popular strains, as he once did with a music-hall ditty, "Nancy Dawson."

When Whitefield left for America in August, 1739, John and Charles were both committed to itinerant preaching after the fashion which Whitefield had set. For the next two or three years they preached in the west and south of England and in Wales, with headquarters at London and Bristol. During the first months, John's preaching was attended with singular phenomena. These ranged from instances of mass hysteria to what seem to have been cases of dissociated personality. Two excerpts from the *Journal* will suffice.

For May 1, 1739, occurs this entry:

At Baldwin Street [Bristol] my voice could scarce be heard amidst the groanings of some and the cries of others, calling aloud to Him that is "mighty to save". . . .

A Quaker, who stood by, was not a little displeased at the dissimulation of those creatures, and was biting his lips and knitting his brows, when he dropped down as thunderstruck. The agony he was in was even terrible to behold. We besought God not to lay folly to his charge. And he soon lifted up his head, and cried aloud, "Now I know thou art a prophet of the Lord."

On October 25 of the same year, Wesley was sent for to see a woman who had been taken ill the evening before.

She lay on the ground, furiously gnashing her teeth, and after a while roared aloud. It was not easy for three or four persons to

hold her, especially when the name of Jesus was named. We prayed;
the violence of her symptoms ceased, though without a complete
deliverance. . . . [The next day] she began screaming before I came
into the room; then broke out into a horrid laughter, mixed with
blasphemy, grievous to hear. One who from many circumstances
apprehended a preternatural agent to be concerned in this, asking,
"How didst thou dare to enter into a Christian?" was answered,
"She is not a Christian. She is mine." "Dost thou not tremble at
the name of Jesus?" No words followed, but she shrunk back and
trembled exceedingly. Q. "Art thou not increasing thy own damna-
tion?" It was faintly answered, "Aye, aye"; which was followed by
fresh cursing and blaspheming.

My brother coming in, she cried out, "Preacher! Field-preacher!
I don't love field-preaching." This was repeated two hours together,
with spitting, and all the expressions of strong aversion.

We left her at twelve, but called again about noon on *Friday,*
the 26th. And now it was that God showed He heareth the prayer.
All her pangs ceased in a moment: she was filled with peace, and
knew that the son of wickedness was departed from her.

George Whitefield preached with more eloquence and tears
than John Wesley, yet such outbursts did not occur under his
preaching, nor did he approve of them. Charles Wesley, the
poet, was also a passionate preacher; but he discouraged such
scenes. At Newcastle, in 1743, he adopted a simple preventive.
He wrote in his *Journal:*

The first night I preached here, half my words were lost through
their outcries. Last night, before I began, I gave public notice that
whosoever cried, so as to drown my voice, should be carried to the
farthest corner of the room. But my porters had no employment the
whole night; yet the Lord was with us, mightily convincing of sin
and righteousness. I am more and more convinced, the fits were a
device of Satan to stop the course of the gospel. Some very unstill
sisters, who always took care to stand near me, and tried which
should cry loudest, since I had them removed out of my sight, have
been as quiet as lambs.

As might be expected, Samuel Wesley had little patience with such occurrences and carried on a sharp correspondence with his brother concerning them. "Did these agitations," he asked, "ever begin during the use of any collects of the Church? or during the preaching of any sermon that had before been preached within consecrated walls without effect, or during the inculcating any other doctrine besides that of your new birth?"

John Wesley's own conclusions regarding the hysteria which was a product mainly of his preaching were characteristic. He gathered his material in logical fashion and passed upon it with a curious blend of practical insight and theological bias.

In March, 1743, he wrote:

I concluded my second course of visiting, in which I inquired particularly into two things: (I) the case of those who had almost every night the last week cried out aloud during the preaching. . . . As to the former I found:

1. That all of them (I think, not one excepted) were persons in perfect health; and had not been subject to fits of any kind, till they were thus affected.

2. That this had come upon every one of them in a moment, without any previous notice, while they were either hearing the word of God or thinking on what they had heard.

3. That in that moment they dropped down, lost all their strength, and were seized with violent pain.

This they expressed in different manners. Some said they felt just as if a sword was running through them; others, that they thought a great weight lay upon them, as if it would squeeze them into the earth. Some said they were quite choked, so that they could not breathe; others, that their hearts swelled ready to burst; and others that it was as if their heart, as if their inside, as if their whole body, was tearing all to pieces.

These symptoms I can no more impute to any natural cause than to the Spirit of God. I can make no doubt that it was Satan tearing them, as they were coming to Christ. And hence proceeded those grievous cries, whereby he might design both to discredit the work of God and to affright fearful people from hearing that word whereby their souls might be saved.

In a tract published in 1745 Wesley was willing to admit that the extraordinary scenes which accompanied his early ministry in Bristol could be explained either "on principles of reason or Scripture." He would not give up his supernatural explanation, but maturer judgment added to it a "natural" one:

For, how easy is it to suppose, that a strong, lively and sudden apprehension of the heinousness of sin, the wrath of God, and the bitter pains of eternal death, should affect the body as well as the soul, during the present laws of vital union, should interrupt or disturb the ordinary circulation, and put nature out of its course! Yea, we may question, whether, while this union subsists, it be possible for the mind to be affected, in so violent a degree, without some or other of those bodily symptoms following.

These phenomena belong to the first period of Methodism. They rarely occurred after 1739 under the preaching of the leaders of the movement and rarely then outside of Bristol.

As the manner of their work was without precedent for that century, so the conditions under which the Methodist preached called for unusual methods. The field preacher had to depend upon his wits to defend himself against disturbers and hecklers who felt free to break in upon meetings held outside of consecrated walls. Wesley's first visit to Bath, the fashionable watering place of the period, was marked by an encounter with Beau Nash, social arbiter of the city. Nash had boasted of his intention to prevent the evangelist preaching, and as a result a large crowd was on hand, including "many of the rich and great." Wesley preached in the plain fashion which he always adopted when speaking to the rich, and with some effect. His own account continues:

Many of them seemed to be a little surprised, and were sinking apace into seriousness, when their champion appeared, and, coming close to me, asked by what authority I did these things. I replied, "By the authority of Jesus Christ, conveyed to me by the (now) Archbishop of Canterbury, when he laid hands upon me, and said, 'Take thou authority to preach the gospel.'" He said, "This is contrary to Act of Parliament: this is a conventicle." I answered, "Sir, the conventicles mentioned in that Act (as the preamble shows) are seditious meetings; but this is not such; here is no shadow of sedition; therefore it is not contrary to that Act." He replied, "I say it is; and, beside, your preaching frightens people out of their wits." "Sir, did you ever hear me preach?" "No." "How, then, can you judge of what you never heard?" "Sir, by common report." "Common report is not enough. Give me leave, sir, to ask, Is not your name Nash?" "My name is Nash." "Sir, I dare not judge of you by common report: I think it not enough to judge by." Here he paused awhile, and, having recovered himself, said, "I desire to know what this people comes here for": on which one replied, "Sir, leave him to me; let an old woman answer him. You, Mr. Nash, take care of your body; we take care of our souls: and for the food of our souls we come here." He replied not a word, but walked away.

Wesley's public preaching was supplemented by personal interviews carried on with friends or chance companions. In June, 1741, he tells of an experiment which illustrates what must have been his common practice:

For these two days I had made an experiment which I had been so often and earnestly pressed to do; speaking to none concerning the things of God, unless my heart was free to it. And what was the event? Why (1) That I spoke to none at all for four-score miles together; no, not even to him that travelled with me in the chaise, unless a few words at first setting out. (2) That I had no cross either to bear or to take up, and commonly in an hour or two fell fast asleep. (3) That I had much respect shown me wherever I came; every one behaving to me as to a civil, good-natured gentleman. Oh how pleasing is all this to flesh and blood! Need ye "compass sea and land" to make "proselytes" to this?

Sometimes Wesley's success in a personal interview was due to other causes than his logic.

I overtook a serious man [May, 1742], with whom I immediately fell into conversation. He presently gave me to know what his opinions were; therefore I said nothing to contradict them. But that did not content him; he was quite uneasy to know whether I held the doctrine of the decrees as he did; but I told him over and over, "We had better keep to practical things, lest we should be angry at one another." And so we did for two miles, till he caught me unawares and dragged me into the dispute before I knew where I was. He then grew warmer and warmer; told me I was rotten at heart, and supposed I was one of John Wesley's followers. I told him, "No, I am John Wesley himself." Upon which—

Improvisum aspris veluti qui sentibus anguem
Pressit—

he would glady have run away outright. But, being the better mounted of the two, I kept close to his side, and endeavoured to show him his heart, till we came into the street of Northampton.

The work could be no longer confined to London and Bristol. In May, 1742, Wesley was called north to attend a dying friend and decided to take this opportunity to go as far as Newcastle upon Tyne, where he had been repeatedly urged to come in order that he might preach to the colliers there as he had preached to the colliers at Kingswood, near Bristol. At seven in the morning, Sunday, May 30, 1742, Wesley walked down into the "poorest and most contemptible part" of Newcastle and with a friend began to sing the hundredth psalm. He preached to the crowd that gathered and announced at the end of the sermon: "If you desire to know who I am, my name is John Wesley. At five in the evening, with God's help, I design to preach here again." Thus began Wesley's work in the apex of that triangle which was to circumscribe the major portion of his activity for the next half century, a triangle of which the points were London, Bristol, Newcastle upon Tyne.

The journeyings which now began were to continue for the rest of the great itinerant's life. Although mainly in the regions defined by his three headquarters, they were by no means limited to this territory; Scotland, Ireland, and Wales were also parts of the Methodist parish over which Wesley had assumed personal supervision. The record of almost any year during his active ministry may be chosen as illustration of the extent of his labors. In January, 1747, for example, Wesley was in Bristol; in February he visited Lincolnshire; during March, April, and May he traveled in Yorkshire and the Midlands; London, Bristol, and Plymouth occupied his attention in June; July he spent in Cornwall; in August he journeyed through Wales to Ireland, returning to Wales in September; and he concluded his year's work in and around London. In such manner he traveled four or five thousand miles a year. Several times he accomplished what was then almost incredible distances in a day's journey—seventy or eighty miles—at least once he went as far as ninety miles in twenty hours.

At least until 1773, that is, until he was seventy, Wesley rode almost altogether on horseback. Turnpikes had not been built in northern England, and there were but few anywhere. Roads were unspeakably bad, and streams were often dangerous for the crude ferries. In October, 1743, Wesley crossed the Trent. His plain record speaks eloquently of the dangers of eighteenth-century travel:

At Ferry we were at a full stop, the boatmen telling us we could not pass the Trent: it was as much as our lives were worth to put from shore before the storm abated. We waited an hour; but, being afraid it would do much hurt if I should disappoint the congregation at Grimsby, I asked the men if they did not think it possible to get to the other shore. They said they could not tell; but if we would venture our lives they would venture theirs. So we put off, having six men, two women, and three horses in the boat. Many stood looking after us on the river-side, in the middle of which we were, when, in an instant, the side of the boat was under water, and the horses and men rolling one over another. We expected the boat to sink every moment; but I did not doubt of being able to swim ashore. The boatmen were amazed, as well as the rest; but they quickly recovered and rowed for life. And soon after, our horses leaping overboard lightened the boat, and we all came un-hurt to land.

A note from a later date will be further illustration of the discomforts of the itinerant. In February, 1747, Wesley was traveling in Lincolnshire.

I was wondering, the day before, at the mildness of the weather; such as seldom attends me in my journeys. But my wonder now ceased: the wind was turned full north, and blew so exceeding hard and keen that when we came to Hatfield neither my companions nor I had much use of our hands or feet. After resting an hour, we bore up again, through the wind and snow, which drove full in our faces. But this was only a squall. In Baldock Field the storm began in earnest. The large hail drove so vehemently in our faces that we could not see, nor hardly breathe. . . . About six I preached to a serious congregation.

On the next morning the servant told Wesley that there could be no traveling that day, as the roads were filled with snow. Wesley replied: "At least we can walk twenty miles a day, with our horses in our hands."

To the physical labor of travel must be added Wesley's exertions in preaching. Again one can turn at random to the *Journal* for the formidable record of his activities. On Sunday, November 28, 1742, he preached at five and at eight in the morning at Newcastle; he then walked seven miles to Tanfield Lea, and after preaching there returned to preach at Newcastle again at four. But preaching three, four, or five times a day was not merely a Sunday exercise. During the week of April 20, 1747, for example, Wesley preached fifteen times in thirteen different places. In fifty years he is supposed to have preached forty thousand sermons.

Year after year Wesley persisted in these labors, lured oftentimes by the news of some village where he had not preached. In his *Journal* appear many such entries as the following: "Having been informed there were many large collieries three or four miles north or north-west from Durham, I rode to a village called Renton, in the midst of them, and proclaimed 'The Lord God, gracious and merciful.'" Or again: "I had had for some time a great desire to go and publish the love of God our Saviour, if it were but for one day, in the Isles of Scilly. . . . So . . . John Nelson, Mr. Shepherd, and I, with three men and a pilot, sailed from St. Ives." But wherever Wesley preached once, there he tried to return, to inspire his societies, to receive new members, to restore the erring, and to expel the recalcitrant. During the '40's Charles traveled almost as constantly as John, but it was John who continued decade after decade in the endless visitation and revisitation. So unceasingly, indeed, did John go about his work that, before the end of the first ten years of his ministry, there were few towns or villages from Tyne to Lands End, from the Welsh mountains to London, which were not accustomed to the sight of a trim clergyman who rode quietly through their streets and who raised his clear voice in the churchyard or at the market cross.

CHAPTER VI

Contra Mundum

Opposition to the new religious movement was inevitable. Both the conditions of the country and the character of the Methodist revival made opposition certain. The invasion of Methodist preachers was resented by high and low alike, but while the bishops replied with quartos, the mob resorted to clubs and stones. The whole story throws a flood of light on social and intellectual conditions in the middle of the century.

England in the 1740's was yet an island of isolated communities. The period of road building had not yet begun, and newspapers were but rarely circulated beyond the city in which they were published. Dwellers in one part of England were "foreigners" to those living in another part. Dialects, which even today are easily distinguished, were then real barriers between communities. As a consequence communication between different parts of England was rare. In 1753 no stagecoach left Liverpool for any other town than London, and that journey occupied four days. Not until 1774 was service between Liverpool and Manchester instituted, and then only for three times a week. One historian declares that in London itself the inhabitants who lived west of Temple Bar differed as much from those who lived on the Essex side of the city as they now do from the peasants of Brittany or the western Pyrenees.

So, too, the parish priest, who by the social organization of the time was an integral part of the governmental as well as of the religious system, was removed, as were his people, from the broader national currents of thought and interest. Only exceptional men like Samuel Wesley retained in secluded parishes active occupation with national policies of the church, and after the discontinuance of convocation in 1722, even their participation was impossible. The parish priest was undisturbed by other than local controversies "and did not vex himself if the Bishops were Arians or Deists. He saw very little of Bishops: he did not know them; and they thought it sufficient if they knew a Duke." Removed from outside interests, the local ministry was keenly sensitive to its pre-eminence in the parish and did not easily brook invasion of its established rights.

The essence of English piety in the eighteenth century was decency and moderation, and in nothing more than in religion did the pious Englishman ask for privacy, for the home was the center of religious life. If in church he paid due respects to religion "as by law established," in his own home he was expected to be the dutiful husband, loving father, and loyal son of the church which his tombstone would celebrate.

For an understanding of the Englishman's mind in the 1740's, one must remember also that this was a particularly nervous decade. Fear of invasion by the French and of an uprising in favor of the Pretender gave the government many a bad night. In 1745 the uprising actually came, but the excitement caused by it was out of all proportion to the real danger. The slightest suspicious action rendered one liable to arrest. Charles Wesley was once arrested on the charge of having prayed for the Pretender. When he was arraigned, he discovered that the only evidence against him was that he had been heard to pray that the Lord "would call home his banished." He explained that he was using figurative language, praying that those who were pilgrims and strangers in the earth might be at home in heaven, and was released.

An uprising of Roman Catholics was especially dreaded, since their cause was supposed to be that of the Pretender, then domiciled in Rome. Popular opinion in the eighteenth century may be inferred from the exclamation of Mrs. Sullen in Farquhar's play, who, when she discovered that she had been robbed, aroused the house with cries of, "Thieves! Murther! Popery!"

In such conditions the Methodists began to preach. Unrelated to the ordered machinery of the Establishment, they went into parishes without leave of anyone. The Wesleys and Whitefield —and later some others—were priests of the Church of England; but their actions raised grave ecclesiastical questions. In 1742 Wesley went to Epworth and, remaining over Sunday, called on the curate, offering to assist either by preaching or by reading prayers. The curate declined the offer and preached a sermon in which he descanted "in a very florid and oratorical manner" against religious "enthusiasm." At the conclusion of the service one of Wesley's friends announced at the church door that "Mr. Wesley, not being permitted to preach in the church, designs to preach here at six o'clock." Wesley's own description of his service is a Methodist classic:

Accordingly at six I came, and found such a congregation as I believe Epworth never saw before. I stood near the east end of the church, upon my father's tombstone, and cried, "The kingdom of heaven is not meat and drink; but righteousness, and peace, and joy in the Holy Ghost."

This is justly considered an epochal scene in Methodist history. Wesley had before this broken parish boundaries and invaded other men's spiritual territory, but this scene gripped popular imagination and became the symbol of Wesley's motto "I look upon all the world as my parish." His right thus to disregard the authority of a legally appointed ecclesiastic in his own parish was justified by Wesley both by ingenious interpretation of canon law and on the grounds of expediency. In August, 1739, he had an interview with the famous Joseph Butler, Bishop of Bristol. To Wesley's explanation of his work the bishop dryly replied: "Very extraordinary, indeed! Well, sir, since you ask my advice, I will give it you very freely. You have no business here; you are not commissioned to preach in this diocese. Therefore I advise you to go hence." Wesley argued that he was a priest of the Church universal, and, being ordained as fellow of a college, he was not limited to any particular cure. "My lord," he said, "my business on earth is to do what good I can. Wherever, therefore, I think I can do most good there must I stay, so long as I think so. At present I think I can do most good here; therefore, here I stay."

Thus Wesley defied the Church of England in the name of the Church of England. To churchmen not troubled as Wesley was by the haunting sense of a mission to be fulfilled and a gospel to preach, such conduct was destructive of all law and order. Less than three weeks before his death John's elder brother, torn by the distress of a loyal Churchman, wrote from Tiverton to his mother:

It was with exceeding concern and grief, I heard you had countenanced a spreading delusion, so far as to be one of Jack's congregation. Is it not enough that I am bereft of both my brothers, but must my mother follow too? . . . They design separation. They are already forbidden all the pulpits in London; and to preach in that diocese is actual schism. In all likelihood, it will come to the same all over England, if the bishops have courage enough. . . . As I told Jack, I am not afraid the Church should excommunicate him (discipline is at too low an ebb), but that he should excommunicate the Church.

In Wesley's own connection he took good care that none of his preachers should interpret the motto "I look upon all the world as my parish" as authority to go where they were not authorized, and in the Methodist Church today there is no greater ecclesiastical offense than that of disregarding another minister's parish rights. But in the meantime Wesley followed in the footsteps of all great reformers who have dared to break institutions in the name of the higher authority of an inner compulsion.

This invasion of parishes despite the wishes of the incumbent was especially offensive owing to the manner and message of the itinerant preacher. As Lecky put it:

The Methodist preacher came to an Anglican parish in the spirit, and with the language, of a missionary going to the most ignorant heathens; and asked the clergyman of the parish to lend him his pulpit, in order that he might instruct the parishioners—perhaps for the first time—in the true gospel of Christ.

And the manner of this instruction and the results of it were all against the grain of traditional English piety. A religion which implied mingling with the mob or exposing one's religious sentiments in public was as revolting as would have been the thought of exposing one's household privacy in the market square. The society meetings upon which Wesley laid so much stress, the love feasts and public testimonies, as well as extravagant emotional scenes, were repugnant alike to the minister and to the respectable part of his congregation. Besides, many of the helpers were crude in their speech, offending sensitive ears by voice and manner. For all these things Wesley cared nothing at all and cried out that the churches were not Christian because they could not distinguish between social exclusiveness, English reserve, and religion. In retaliation the clergy locked their doors, and the gentry, with those who wanted to be taken for gentry, tried not to smile when they heard that the mob had attacked a Methodist preacher.

At first thought the Methodists would seem to be the last people to be suspected as "papists," but this was a common charge. The High Churchmanship of the Oxford Club and the complaints of the Georgians against Wesley's rigorousness in enforcing the canons which more prudent Churchmen had allowed to fall into desuetude help to explain the suspicion. But Wesley also showed a more tolerant spirit toward the Catholics than did his contemporaries, and the loose talk of the Methodists about dreams and visions reminded men of similar claims made by medieval monks, and they hastened to draw the parallel. The Bishop of Exeter wrote a ponderous volume on *The Enthusiasm of Methodists and Papists Compared,* Hogarth drew a cartoon of a Methodist preacher with the shaven crown of a friar under his wig, and Horace Walpole voiced a general suspicion when he "apprehended" that "the Methodists are secret Papists."

Other causes of opposition must be recognized. The puritanic character of the Methodists and their doctrines made them unpopular with many. The tavernkeeper was at one with the actor and the beau in disliking Wesley and his followers. The fox-hunting, hard-drinking country parson would not look with favor upon a brother priest who referred publicly to "soul-damning clergymen." The village loafer and the squire alike would squirm at the liberal promises of fire and brimstone which were voiced at the market cross in a day when hell was not as yet explained away. To the upper classes Wesley was particularly irritating, for his diatribes could not be ignored by a tolerant audience willing to patronize a popular preacher. Wesley would not be patronized. His consciousness of being wellborn and fellow of a college prevented his accepting the condescensions of people of his own class.[1] As a result denuncia-

[1] "John Wesley, the gentleman, had a peculiar dislike for the fashionable world, in which Whitefield, the pot-boy, was peculiarly happy." A. J. Mason, "John Wesley, A Lecture" *The Church Historical Society Publications,* XLVI, (London, 1908), p. 34.

tions of the rich and great which were but part of the sauce for polite companies meeting in the Countess of Huntingdon's parlors to hear Whitefield became personal insults when spoken by Wesley. His puritanism could not be excused; it was a betrayal of his class.

Opposition to Methodism took many forms. Several hundred anti-Methodist publications of the time are in one collection in America. Beside the publications of the clergy there were more or less extended references by playwrights and novelists who hoped to get a laugh at the expense of the disliked Methodists. Samuel Foote was especially prolific in this regard, no less than nine of his plays making mention of the Methodists; one, *The Minor*, contained extended ridicule. As early as 1743 Wesley was in Newcastle when a play called *Trick upon Trick, or Methodism Displayed* was advertised. In his *Journal*, Wesley gave details of the performance, evidently relishing the outcome.

On *Friday* a vast multitude of spectators were assembled in the Moot Hall to see this. It was believed there could not be less than fifteen hundred people, some hundreds of whom sat on rows of seats built upon the stage. Soon after the comedians had begun the first act of the play, on a sudden all those seats fell down at once, the supporters of them breaking like a rotten stick. The people were thrown one upon another, about five foot forward, but not one of them hurt. After a short time the rest of the spectators were quiet, and the actors went on. In the middle of the second act all the shilling seats gave a crack and sunk several inches down. A great noise and shrieking followed; and as many as could readily get to the door went out and returned no more. Notwithstanding this, when the noise was over, the actors went on with the play. In the beginning of the third act the entire stage suddenly sunk about six inches. The players retired with great precipitation; yet in a while they began again. At the latter end of the third act all the sixpenny seats, without any kind of notice, fell to the ground. There was now a cry on every side, it being supposed that many were crushed in pieces; but, upon inquiry, not a single person (such was the mercy of God!) was either killed or dangerously hurt. Two or three hundred remaining still in the hall, Mr. Este (who was to act the Methodist) came upon the stage and told them, for all this, he was resolved the farce should be acted. While he was speaking the stage sunk six inches more; on which he ran back in the utmost confusion, and the people as fast as they could out of the door, none staying to look behind him.

Which is most surprising—that those players acted this farce the next week, or that some hundreds of people came again to see it?

Among the novelists Fielding ridiculed the Methodists in *Joseph Andrews* and *Amelia* and Smollett caricatured them in *The Expedition of Humphry Clinker.* It was assumed in such circles that Methodists were either mad or hypocrites, the latter explanation being favored.

Ridicule was not the only weapon used by the adversaries of Wesley. In excited times an excitable populace was not likely to rest content with literary allusions. Whether the mob was in holiday mood or otherwise, made little difference for the luckless Methodists. Wesley was once pelted by a mob in Leeds which was celebrating the choice of the Duke of Tuscany as emperor, and the evangelist tartly observed that the Lord could not give the English nation the blessings he would because in celebration they would tear their countrymen to pieces.

The excitement which reigned in '45, especially in the north of England, which lay in constant fear of invasion from Scotland, is movingly described in Wesley's *Journal;* for he was in Newcastle in September, 1745. The town was under heavy guard, and several of the gates had been walled up. In the midst of the turmoil Wesley wrote a characteristic letter to the mayor, assuring him of the loyalty of the Methodists and suggesting that something should be done about open vice in the city. Then, while cannon were mounted on the walls and the people carried out their goods, Wesley preached on "the wisdom of God in governing the world."

There was no trouble for the Methodists at Newcastle, but the scene is typical of the way in which Wesley moved quietly in the midst of tumult, although he did not always come off so well. Clergymen and gentry were not above inciting the mob against a Methodist preacher, and the mob, panicky at the whisper of "popery" or "treason," was not easy to quell, once its fears were aroused.

At Gwennap, in Wales, two gentlemen with a press gang forced themselves through the congregation where Wesley was preaching, and ordered their men to seize some of the auditors. The people, led by Wesley, calmly began a hymn, at which one of the gentlemen cried out, "Seize him, seize him! I say, seize the preacher for his Majesty's service." When his men did not move, he seized Wesley by the cassock and cried, "I take you to serve his Majesty." Wesley's account follows:

A servant taking his horse, he took me by the arm, and we walked arm-in-arm for about three-quarters of a mile. He entertained me all the time with the "wickedness of the fellows belonging to the society." When he was taking breath I said, "Sir, be they what they will, I apprehend it will not justify you in seizing me in this manner, and violently carrying me away, as you said, to serve his Majesty." He replied, *"I seize you! And violently carry you away!* No, sir; no. Nothing like it. I asked you to go with me to my house, and you said you was willing; and if so, you are welcome; and if not, you are welcome to go where you please." I answered, "Sir, I know not if it would be safe for me to go back through this rabble." "Sir," said he, "I will go with you myself." He then called for his horse, and another for me, and rode back with me to the place from whence he took me.

Every effort was made to interfere with Methodist meetings. Drummers marched through the audience; cattle were driven into the open-air meetings. A harlequin once climbed a pole in Moorfields, when Whitefield was preaching, and attempted by indecent actions to draw attention from the preacher. But Methodist preachers were skilled in overcoming such interruptions. The audiences gave way before the drummers and closed behind them again; the cattle were driven off. Even the harlequin was made the basis of scathing remarks concerning the nature of the opposers. The Methodists met more than interruption, however; and the preachers often stood in danger of their lives.

No secondhand accounts will take the place of the records of the *Journal,* for Wesley's concise English is admirably adapted to describe stirring scenes in which he was chief actor. His own courage stands out the clearer for his apparent unconsciousness of it.

At Falmouth, Wesley was calling on a sick woman.

Almost as soon as I was set down [he says], the house was beset on all sides by an innumerable multitude of people. A louder or more confused noise could hardly be at the taking of a city by storm. At first Mrs. B. and her daughter endeavored to quiet them; but it was labour lost. They might as well have attempted to still the raging of the sea. They were soon glad to shift for themselves, and leave K.E. and me to do as well as we could. The rabble roared with all their throats, "Bring out the Canorum! Where is the Canorum?" (an unmeaning word which the Cornish generally use instead of Methodist). No answer being given, they quickly forced open the outer door and filled the passage. Only a wainscot-partition was between us, which was not likely to stand long. I immediately took down a large looking-glass which hung against it, supposing the whole side would fall in at once. When they began their work, with abundance of bitter imprecations, poor Kitty was utterly astonished, and cried out, "O sir, what must we do?" I said, "We must pray." Indeed at that time, to all appearance, our lives were not worth an hour's purchase. She asked, "But, sir, is it not better for you to hide yourself? To get into the closet?" I answered, "No. It is best for me to stand just where I am." Among those without were the crews of some privateers, which were lately come into the harbour. Some of these, being angry at the slowness of the rest, thrust them away, and, coming up altogether, set their shoulders to the inner door, and cried out, "Avast, lads, avast!" Away went all the hinges at once, and the door fell back into the room. I stepped forward at once into the midst of them, and said, "Here I am. Which of you has anything to say to me? To which of you have I done any wrong? To you? Or you? Or you?" I continued speaking till I came, bare-headed as I was (for I purposely left my hat, that they might all see my face), into the middle of the street, and then, raising my voice, said, "Neighbours, countrymen! Do you desire to hear me speak?" They cried vehemently, "Yes, yes. He shall speak. He shall. Nobody shall hinder him." But having nothing to stand on, and no advantage of ground, I could be heard by few only. However, I spoke without intermission, and, as far as the sound reached, the people were still; till one or two of their captains turned about and swore not a man should touch him.

In a neighboring parish Wesley was saved from a similar scene only by the intervention of an Oxford friend, and was told it was rumored that he had been for a long time in France and Spain and was sent to England by the Pretender. He was also told that one of the gentry had declared publicly "in the face of the whole congregation, as they were coming out of the church, 'If any man of this parish dares to hear these fellows, he shall not come to my Christmas feast!'"

At Wednesbury, in October, 1743, the house in which Wesley was lodging was beset by a mob. After a while, with the little group praying in the house, the mob dispersed. Wesley thought it wise to go, but remained out of deference to the wishes of his friends. The mob came again, and Wesley succeeded in calming them, proferring to go with them to any magistrate. They went to two, who refused to see them. Returning, the Wednesbury mob was met and overpowered by a mob from the village of Walsall.

To attempt speaking was vain [runs Wesley's account of what followed], for the noise on every side was like the roaring of the sea. So they dragged me along till we came to the town, where, seeing the door of a large house open, I attempted to go in; but a man, catching me by the hair, pulled me back into the middle of the mob. They made no more stop till they had carried me through the main street, from one end of the town to the other. I continued speaking all the time to those within hearing, feeling no pain or weariness. At the west end of the town, seeing a door half open, I made toward it, and would have gone in, but a gentleman in the shop would not suffer me, saying they would pull the house down to the ground. However, I stood at the door and asked, "Are you willing to hear me speak?" Many cried out, "No, no! knock his brains out; down with him; kill him at once." Others said, "Nay, but we will hear him first." I began asking, "What evil have I done? Which of you all have I wronged in word or deed?" and continued speaking for above a quarter of an hour, till my voice suddenly failed. Then the floods began to lift up their voice again, many crying out, "Bring him away! Bring him away!"

In the meantime my strength and my voice returned, and I broke out aloud into prayer. And now the man who just before headed the mob turned and said, "Sir, I will spend my life for you: follow me, and not one soul here shall touch a hair of your head." Two or three of his fellows confirmed his words, and got close to me immediately. At the same time, the gentleman in the shop cried out, "For shame, for shame! Let him go." An honest butcher, who was a little farther off, said it was a shame they should do thus; and pulled back four or five, one after another, who were running on the most fiercely. The people then, as if it had been by common consent, fell back to the right and left; while those three or four men took me between them, and carried me through them all. But on the bridge the mob rallied again: we therefore went on one side over the mill-dam, and thence through the meadows, till, a little before ten, God brought me safe to Wednesbury, having lost only one flap of my waistcoat and a little skin from one of my hands.

True to his habit, Wesley reviewed the happenings of that night, finding in them a remarkable "chain of providences" and analyzing his own mental reactions. He had not stumbled when to have fallen under the feet of the mob would have been death, the flap of his waistcoat which contained a bank note had been only half torn off, and a man who had rushed at him with his arm raised had only stopped, stroked Wesley's head, and said, "What soft hair he has!" For himself Wesley had been perfectly calm, taking no thought "for one moment before another." Once he had thought that, if they threw him into the river, the papers in his pocket would be ruined; but he had no fear, since he was sure that he could swim across in safety, clothed as he was.

John Wesley was not alone in braving the attacks of mobs. Only five days after his brother's experience in Wednesbury, Charles Wesley preached to the little congregation there, where Methodist houses were marked by broken windowpanes. The lay preachers were even more subject to attack, since their manners were cruder and their presumption in preaching more resented. Contemporary accounts of their sermons from unsympathetic hands would indicate that there must have been in the sermons of the helpers much that was offensive to good taste. If so, the preachers paid dearly for the offense. James Wheatley was dragged by the hair through the streets of Norwich. Moses Dale was carried around Northwich on a butcher's block, set down in the market place and cow horns blown into his ears until he was almost deafened. Others were pressed as soldiers or had their houses torn down and their families abused. Wesley was proud of his preachers. "For what pay," he asked, "could we procure men to do this service—to be always ready to go to prison or to death?"

Sometimes the rioters fell into their own pit. At Bolton, Wesley was preaching in spite of flying stones, when one of his tormentors, bawling at his ear, was struck by a stone. Another was hit in the forehead. A third stretched out his hand for the preacher and was hit on the knuckle with a sharp rock. Wesley says that "he shook his hand, and was very quiet till I concluded my discourse and went away." In Ireland, Wesley often found uninvited, but appreciated, champions who used other than the weapons of the Spirit. At one place three interrupters were stilled, the first two by people leading the disturbers away; the third, a noisy man, was floored by a butcher—"not one of the Methodists," said Wesley, adding, "so I quietly finished my discourse."

Appeal to the authorities was often useless; they were either unwilling or unable to act. Wesley's protest to the mayor of Cork, in 1750, was as cutting as it was short. He wrote:

I fear God and honour the king. I earnestly desire to be at peace with all men. I have not willingly given any offence either to the magistrates, the clergy, or any of the inhabitants of the city of Cork, neither do I desire anything of them but to be treated, I will not say as a clergyman, a gentleman, or a Christian, but with such justice and humanity as are due to a Jew, a Turk, or a pagan.

The ecclesiastical courts, as Samuel Wesley had predicted, were slow to proceed against the Methodists. The more fiery of the bishops were content to issue pamphlets against Methodist enthusiasm, while the others were perhaps as little disposed to welcome troublesome complaints as troublesome Methodists. An Irish clergyman was wont to protest to Archbishop Ryder, of Tuam, about the Methodism of Walter Shirley. Once he hastened to the Archbishop, saying, "O, your Grace, I have such a circumstance to communicate to you, one that will astonish you!" To the Archbishop's inquiry he replied with his new charge against Shirley: "Why, my lord, he wears—white stockings."

"Very anticlerical and very dreadful, indeed," answered the prelate; and drawing his chair closer to the informer, he asked, "Does Mr. Shirley wear them over his boots?"

"No, your Grace."

"Well, sir," advised Ryder, "the first time you find him with his stockings over his boots, pray inform me; and I shall deal accordingly with him."

The secular courts were as slow to protect as the ecclesiastical courts were slow to prosecute the Methodists. In the inferior courts, indeed, the magistrates were often hostile; but Wesley at last appealed to the superior courts and found protection. In 1749 he declared: "There is one, and only one way—move the King's Bench for information against them. This is a way which has never failed us yet." While local difficulties continued until well into the nineteenth century, the Wesleys themselves were more and more relieved from danger of mob violence. This Wesley attributed to the policy of the Crown. But the truth is that while local Methodist preachers could yet expect the solicitous attentions of boisterous spirits, Wesley and his brother gradually won a grudging respect, so that in later years the leaders were but little molested.

CHAPTER VII

"Pope John"

THE practical problems of organizing his work drove Wesley back to the methods to which he was committed by temperament as well as by conviction. In the Oxford Club, Wesley had an organization which with modification proved useful both in the university and in America. His new interest in personal, mystical religion led him to shift somewhat his own conception of the aim of such a society; but he never lost faith in the idea of a methodical, regulated association of seekers after holiness. The old religious societies, including his own Oxford Club, did not satisfy him, because they lacked the mystical note. The Moravians had disappointed him, both because of what he considered their extreme mysticism and because they seemed to him unsympathetic with his own Church of England. He now asked himself: Could not societies be organized on the Oxford plan of promoting personal religion and yet be open to both churchmen and dissenters alike? Could not such a religious society invite everyone—regardless of his theology—who was converted or who was "groaning so to be"?

Wesley's answer to these questions was his organization of the Methodist societies. The proposal to disregard the barriers of church and of orthodoxy was in itself so daring as to be revolutionary. "I am sick of opinions," said Wesley; and he insisted, as early as 1742, that the distinguishing marks of a Methodist "are not his opinions of any sort, his assenting to this or that scheme of religion, his embracing any particular set of notions, his espousing the judgment of one man or another." To his conference he put his view as to theological differences in untheological language:

I have no more right to object to a man for holding a different opinion from mine than I have to differ with a man because he wears a wig and I wear my own hair; but if he take his wig off and shakes the powder in my eyes, I shall consider it my duty to get quit of him as soon as possible.

The rules which governed his societies, adopted at the beginning of his work, state that the sole requirement for admission is a "desire to flee from the wrath to come, to be saved from their sins." In extreme old age he reaffirmed this position from which he had never deviated:

One circumstance more is quite peculiar to the people called Methodists: that is, the terms upon which any person may be admitted to their society: They do not impose, in order to their admission, any opinions whatsoever. Let them hold particular or general redemption, absolute or conditional decrees: let them be Churchmen, or Dissenters, Presbyterians or Independents, it is no obstacle. Let them choose one mode of baptism or another, it is no bar to their admission. The Presbyterian may be a Presbyterian still; the Independent and Anabaptist use his own mode of worship. So may the Quaker; and none will contend with him about it. They think and let think.

To create such a society in a century in which denominational lines were political as well as theological would seem to have been a hopeless task, but to this task Wesley brought a genius for organization. He began by organizing small groups on the model of the Oxford Club and the religious societies which he and his brother had organized in Georgia. Then, by chance, in providing for a debt incurred in building a meeting place in Bristol, he hit upon a plan for close supervision of the societies in his absence. Leaders originally appointed to collect a penny a week from each member who could pay were charged also with looking after the moral and spiritual condition of the membership. Soon every member of the societies belonged to special groups for confession or for "testimony" and was under direct and careful supervision.

If uniformity of opinion was not required of the Methodists, uniformity of conduct was. The General Rules, which have been preserved in the Methodist Church today, indicate the kind of life which was considered methodistic:

There is only one condition previously required in those who desire admission into these Societies [so run the Rules], *a desire to flee from the wrath to come, to be saved from their sins.* But wherever this is really fixed in the soul, it will be shown by its fruits. It is therefore expected of all who continue therein, that they should continue to evidence their desire of salvation,

First, by doing no harm; by avoiding evil in every kind; especially that which is most generally practiced. Such is:

The taking the name of God in vain;

The profaning the day of the Lord, either by doing ordinary work thereon, or by buying or selling;

Drunkenness, *buying or selling spirituous liquors;* or *drinking them* (unless in cases of extreme necessity) ;

Fighting, quarrelling, brawling; *going to law;* returning evil for evil or railing for railing; the *using many words* in buying or selling;

The buying or selling uncustomed goods;

The giving or taking things on usury;

Uncharitable or unprofitable conversation;

Doing to others as we would not they should do unto us;

Doing what we know is not for the glory of God: as

The *putting on of gold, or costly apparel;*

The *taking such diversions* as cannot be used in the name of the Lord Jesus;

The *singing* those *songs,* or *reading* those *books,* which do not tend to the knowledge or love of God;

Softness, and needless self-indulgence;

Laying up treasures upon earth.

It is expected of all who continue in these Societies that they should continue to evidence their desire of salvation,

Secondly, By doing good; by being, in every kind, merciful after their power; as they have opportunity, doing good of every possible sort, and as far as possible, to all men:

To their bodies, of the ability which God giveth, by giving food to the hungry, by clothing the naked, by visiting or helping them that are sick, or in prison:

To their souls, by instructing, *reproving,* or exhorting all we have any intercourse with; trampling underfoot that enthusiastic doctrine of devils, that "we are not to do good unless *our heart is free to it.*"

By doing good, especially, to them that are of the household of faith, or groaning so to be; employing them preferably to others, buying one of another, helping each other in business; and that so much the more because the world will love its own, and them only.

By all possible *diligence and frugality,* that the gospel be not blamed.

By running with patience the race that is set before them; *denying themselves* and taking up their cross daily; submitting to bear the reproach of Christ, to be as the filth and offscouring of the world; and that men should *say all manner of evil of them falsely, for their Lord's sake.*

It is expected of all who desire to continue in these Societies that they should continue to evidence their desire of salvation,

Thirdly, By attending upon all the ordinances of God; such are:

The public worship of God;

The ministry of the word, either read or expounded;

The supper of the Lord;

Private prayer;

Searching the Scriptures; and fasting, or abstinence.

Some of these rules were not easily kept by the Methodists. The rule against smuggled goods was especially distasteful to societies in southern England where smuggling was a respectable occupation. On these points Wesley made no compromise with the feelings of his members, and his method of dealing with his followers appears in his tract, *A Word to a Smuggler*. "Open smuggling," he wrote, "is robbing on the highway. . . . A smuggler of this kind is no honester than a highwayman. They may shake hands together. Private smuggling is just the same with picking of pockets."

His rule with regard to gold and costly apparel caused even more difficulty because the temptation to violate it was more widespread. In *Advice to the People called Methodists, with Regard to Dress,* Wesley interpreted his rule in unmistakable language:

Wear no gold, (whatever officers of state may do; or magistrates, as the ensign of their office,) no pearls, or precious stones; use no curling of hair, or costly apparel, how grave soever. I advise those who are able to receive this saying, Buy no velvets, no silks, no fine linen, no superfluities, no mere ornaments, though ever so much in fashion. Wear nothing, though you have it already, which is of a glaring colour, or which is in any kind gay, glistening, or showy; nothing made in the very height of the fashion, nothing apt to attract the eyes of the by-standers. I do not advise women to wear rings, ear-rings, necklaces, lace, (of whatever kind or colour,) or ruffles, which, by little and little, may easily shoot out from one to twelve inches deep. Neither do I advise men to wear coloured waist-coats, shining stockings, glittering or costly buckles or buttons, either on their coats, or in their sleeves, any more than gay, fashionable, or expensive perukes.

One of Wesley's chief objections to costly dress was that the money thus used might have been turned to other channels.

If those who do observe them [the Rules], employ the money they thus save in the most excellent manner, then a part of what before only served to fat a few rich tradesmen for hell, will suffice to feed and clothe and employ many poor that seek the kingdom of heaven.

Since he was thinking mainly of the economic phase of the

matter, he did not recommend any uniformity or singularity of dress such as the Quakers used, recommending rather that each individual conform to the custom of his country and times. When taxed with inconsistency in thus advising conformity to the customs of the country, he explained somewhat tartly: "When I appear in public, I am decently appareled, according to my age and the custom of England; sometimes in a short coat, sometimes in a nightgown,[1] sometimes in a gown and cassock."

Wesley's insistence on attendance upon the public worship of God, "the supper of the Lord," and on fasting indicates that the Methodists were expected to maintain a churchly piety consonant with Wesley's High Church beliefs. The remarkable fact is that he was willing for those not communicants of the Church of England to perform these duties in their own churches.

Wesley also undertook to direct the freeholders of his societies in their voting. He not only forbade taking money in return for a vote, but he declared that voter perjured who received entertainment, meat, or drink. His advice to the voter was: "Act as if the whole election depended upon your single vote, and as if the whole Parliament depended (and therein the whole nation) on that single person whom you now choose to be a member of it." A man who loves God should be preferred to all others, but in lieu of such a one—thought Wesley the Tory —a voter should support him "that loves the King, King George." "A King is a lovely, sacred name. He is a Minister of God unto thee for good." To those who said that they voted for the country, not the king, Wesley replied: "Who taught you to separate your King from your country? . . . Is not the interest of the King of England, and of the country of England, one and the same?"

[1] A "dressing gown" in eighteenth-century usage.

Advice as to voting was not confined to tracts, for Wesley personally took a hand in elections, trying to persuade his followers to aid the king's party. In this he was not confined to the Tory interest, but endeavored to support the candidate who was approved by the king. In 1756 the parliamentary election at Bristol was hotly contested, and the Tory candidate, Jarrit Smith, was thought to lean toward the Pretender's cause, while the Whig candidate, John Spencer—afterward Earl Spencer— was favored by the king. Wesley threw his support to Spencer and wrote to a friend concerning the election:

Last night I desired all the freemen of our Society to meet me after preaching, and enlarged a little upon His Majesty's character and the reasons we had to spare no pains in his service. I believe all who had been wavering were fully convinced.

The Methodists seem to have been convinced, but Spencer's opponent was elected.

Even tea drinking came in for attention from the head of the Methodists. Wesley had been convinced that copious drinking of green tea was injurious, especially productive of nervous disorders. For several years he himself left off tea drinking. When he stopped the use of it in the four headquarters, London, Bristol, Kingswood, and Newcastle, he found that he was saving, on these four households, some fifty pounds a year. This was irrefutable argument, so he most strongly advised his people to leave off tea drinking altogether and to apply to charity the money thus saved. In place of tea he recommended warm milk, sage, green balm, mint or pennyroyal tea, anything which would be cheaper and, as he thought, less injurious. For those who feared refusing tea would offend others, Wesley provided a ready-made answer:

If any ask you, simply reply, "I do not drink tea; I never use it." If they say, "Why, you did drink it"; answer, "I did so; but I have left it off a considerable time." Those who have either good nature or good manners will say no more. But if any should impertinently add, "Oh, but why did you leave it off?" answer mildly, "Because I thought water-gruel (suppose) was wholesomer as well as cheaper." If they, with still greater ill-manners and impertinence, go on, "What, you do it because Mr. Wesley bids you"; reply calmly, "True; I do it because Mr. Wesley, on good reasons, advises me so to do." If they add the trite cant phrase, "What, you follow man!" reply, without any emotion, "Yes, I follow any man, you or him or any other, who gives me good reason for so doing." If they persist in cavilling, close the whole matter with, "I neither drink it nor dispute about it."

Yet the Methodists were allowed latitude—at least in theory —where one would least expect it. If Wesley was puritanic in his morals, he had, nevertheless, a tolerance not always credited to puritanism. The Methodist rules were directed against no specific amusements; the only warning was against "taking such diversions as cannot be used in the name of the Lord Jesus." That this is not an oversight appears from Wesley's own words. In one of his sermons he said that he could not himself go to the theater or play cards, but he continued: "Possibly others can: I am not obliged to pass any sentence on them that are otherwise minded. I leave them to their own Master; to Him let them stand or fall." This was Wesley's principle, although in the societies he enforced a stricter and narrower discipline.

Oversight of the Methodists, who were rapidly increasing throughout the British Isles, soon required so much time that he was compelled to employ other preachers. At the suggestion of his mother Wesley allowed a layman, Thomas Maxfield, to preach. The results were so satisfactory that he extended the practice, taking laymen—stonemasons, soldiers, small tradesmen—and using them both to preach and to look after the societies. John Nelson, John Bennet, Thomas Maxfield, and others traveled almost as incessantly as Wesley and preached, if not with equal intelligence, at least with equal fervor. Several of the early preachers were soldiers when converted or were later "pressed" into service, so that Methodist societies were organized in the camps of English troops abroad as well as in England. At the battle of Fontenoy, May 11, 1745, four lay preachers were killed. One of them, Clements by name, had his arm broken by a musket ball. When they would have carried him from the field, he protested that he had yet an arm left to hold his sword. When that arm was shot away, he cried out that he was as happy as he could be out of paradise. Another preacher, John Evans, having both legs shot away by a chain shot, was laid across a cannon to die, where he exhorted as long as he could speak.

Wesley organized his preachers and governed them even more strictly than he did the members. For their guidance he drew up some rules analogous to the General Rules for the societies as a whole:

(1) Be diligent. Never be unemployed a moment. Never be triflingly employed. Never while away time; neither spend any more time at any place than is strictly necessary.

(2) Be serious. Let your motto be, "Holiness to the Lord." Avoid all lightness, jesting, and foolish talking.

(3) Converse sparingly and cautiously with women; particularly with young women.

(4) Take no step toward marriage, without first consulting with your brethren.

(5) Believe evil of no one. . . .

(6) Speak evil of no one. . . .

(7) Tell every one what you think wrong in him. . . .

(8) Do not affect the gentleman. You have no more to do with this character than with that of a dancing master. . . .

(9) Be ashamed of nothing but sin: not of fetching wood (if time permit) or drawing water; not of cleaning your own shoes, or your neighbor's.

(10) Be punctual. Do every thing exactly at the time. And, in general, do not mend our rules, but keep them; not for wrath, but for conscience' sake.

(11) You have nothing to do but to save souls. Therefore spend and be spent in this work. . . .

Observe: It is not your business to preach so many times, and to take care of this or that society; but to save as many souls as you can; to bring as many sinners as you possibly can to repentance, and with all your power to build them up in that holiness without which they cannot see the Lord. And remember! A Methodist preacher is to mind every point, great and small, in the Methodist discipline! Therefore you will need all the sense you have, and to have all your wits about you!

(12) Act in all things, not according to your own will, but as a son in the Gospel. As such, it is your part to employ your time in the manner which we direct; partly, in preaching and visiting from house to house; partly, in reading, meditation, and prayer. Above all, if you labor with us in our Lord's vineyard, it is needful that you should do that part of the work which we advise, at those times and places which we judge most for his glory.

Wesley urged his preachers to spend at least five hours out of the twenty-four in reading. They were not to confine themselves to the Bible, and if they could not buy other books, Wesley agreed to furnish them to the value of five pounds. At London, Bristol, and Newcastle upon Tyne libraries for the preachers were established which included sixteen Latin, twelve Greek writers, and a Hebrew Bible. At the first conference the question was asked, "What books may an Assistant read?" The answer named the Greek Testament and more than a dozen other books in Greek and Latin, Virgil, Horace, Epictetus, Plato, and Homer appearing in the list. One must remember that Wesley's helpers, although chosen mainly from the trades, were not illiterate men. One seventh of the preachers in the connection during Wesley's lifetime eventually took orders in the Establishment, and a careful study of the others shows that most of them had a good general education.

To requirements concerning studies Wesley added detailed instructions as to preaching. A sermon was meant " (1) To invite; (2) To convince; (3) To offer Christ; (4) To build up." "Take care of anything awkward or affected, either in your gesture, phrase, or pronunciation," counseled Wesley. "In repeating the Lord's Prayer, remember to say 'hallowed,' not 'hollowed.' " The preacher should avoid "quaint" words, such as *object, originate*. In spelling the preacher should eschew "the fashionable impropriety" of leaving out the *u* in words like honor and vigor.

Over his preachers Wesley exercised unyielding authority. The conferences were free discussions between Wesley, his lay preachers, and such evangelical clergymen as were interested enough to come; but they were dominated by Wesley himself. A woman observer at one of the conferences quoted a preacher as saying that there was "much concord," but "Mr. Wesley seemed to do all the business himself." Indeed, Wesley would allow no appeal from his authority on the part of either people or preacher. In the "Large Minutes," which were issued and revised from 1744 to 1789, Wesley stated his conception of his own power in no uncertain terms. "What is that power?" he asked.

It is a power of admitting into, and excluding from, the societies under my care; of choosing and removing stewards; of receiving or not receiving helpers; of appointing them when, where, and how to help me, and of desiring any of them to confer with me when I see good.

To objections against his control over the preachers, Wesley answered:

But some of our helpers say, "This is shackling freeborn Englishmen;" and demand a free conference, that is, a meeting of all the preachers, wherein all things shall be determined by most votes. I answer, it is possible, after my death, something of this kind may take place; but not while I live. To me the preachers have engaged themselves to submit, to serve me as sons in the Gospel; but they are not thus engaged to any man or number of men besides. To me the people in general will submit; but they will not thus submit to any other.

It is nonsense, then, to call my using this power, 'shackling free-born Englishmen." None needs to submit to it unless he will; so that there is no shackling in the case. Every preacher and every member may leave me when he pleases. But while he chooses to stay, it is on the same terms that he joined me at first.

This was the attitude that won for Wesley the title of "Pope John."

The judgment of one of Wesley's loyal followers was that no man—not even "St. Paul himself"—ever possessed so much power over so large a body of men. But he added that "from the creation of the world" so large a body had never looked up to any single person with a more profound reverence than did the preachers to John Wesley. In fact, the autocracy of Wesley is but evidence of his ability to command loyalty and to inspire reverence. The Methodist societies were carefully organized, but it was John Wesley who breathed into this organization the breath of life.

His very appearance and demeanor contributed to his influence over men. John Hampson said that "many, who had been greatly prejudiced against him, have been known to change their opinion the moment they were introduced into his presence." He had the ability to make himself at home in any company. "Had he lived in a Court all his days," wrote one who knew Wesley well, "his address could not have been more easy and polite: yet he could be quite content amongst the most homely Tradesmen and Peasants, and suit his Discourse to the meanest capacity." "I hate to meet John Wesley," said Johnson to Boswell; "the dog enchants me with his conversation, and then breaks away to go and see some old woman."

Wesley not only knew how to suit his discourse to the "meanest capacity," but he could also bear hardship along with the sturdiest of his preachers. John Nelson, a former stonemason, was with Wesley on an early preaching tour in Cornwall. They had to sleep on the floor, Wesley using Nelson's greatcoat for a pillow while Nelson laid his head on a copy of Burkitt's *Notes on the New Testament*. Nelson says that after spending nearly three weeks in this way, Wesley one morning about three o'clock clapped him on the shoulder and said: "Brother Nelson, let us be of good cheer. I have one whole side yet, for the skin is off but one side." Nelson remembered that on the same trip Wesley told him that they should be thankful for plenty of blackberries, "for," said he, "this is the best country I ever saw for getting a stomach, but the worst that ever I saw for getting food."

Despite his autocratic method Wesley was able to make the *amende honorable* when he felt it necessary. At a conference Wesley as was his custom called the names of his preachers and asked if there was any complaint against them. In calling the roll, he omitted his own name and that of his brother. One of the preachers rose to object to the president's action. Wesley warmly answered that he would not submit to examination by his preachers. "Then," replied the preacher, "I have done," and sat down. Wesley recovered his poise and called his own name, whereupon the preacher complained that Wesley had often promised to visit his circuit, but had not done so, to the grief of the people. Wesley made no reply until after breakfast. When he returned to the conference, he apologized to the preacher publicly and to the conference for his "improper warmth."

For many years toward the close of Wesley's life, Joseph Bradford was his traveling companion. One day Wesley told Bradford to take some letters to the post. Bradford replied that he would take them after preaching. "Take them now, Joseph," said Wesley. A contention followed, which ended with Wesley saying, "Then you and I must part." In the morning Wesley called Bradford and asked, "Joseph, have you considered what I said, that we must part?"

"Please yourself, sir."

"Will you ask my pardon, Joseph?"

"No, sir."

"You can't?"

"No, sir."

"Then will I yours, Joseph," said Wesley. The truth was that, receiving so much adulation, Wesley appreciated occasional contradiction. "No man in England has contradicted me so much as you have done," he once said to Henry Moore, "and yet I love you still."

Wesley had a stock of humor little suspected today by those who read only his commonly known works. He loved to tell stories, and his varied experiences in Europe and America gave him a fund from which he drew to the delight of many a provincial fireside. No one can estimate the educational value to England of one Oxford don traveling constantly for half a century and always a welcome guest in thousands of homes. Even in his old age the young people loved to hear him, for, as Alexander Knox said, "No cynical remarks on the levity of youth embittered his discourse. No applausive retrospect to past times marked his present discontent."

Grave Thomas Walsh complained that Wesley's proverbs tempted him "to levity." If Wesley in his younger days discouraged laughter as sinful, he must have repented; for his later friends bear unanimous witness that he was the most delightful of companions. Southey observes very justly that Wesley objected to many innocent amusements, forgetting that he himself had no need of such entertainment, since wherever he went, his presence "made a festival among his friends." He was always on the move, meeting new people and revisiting old friends. He did not realize that the stay-at-homes were not so well provided with diversion as he.

His native courtesy often stood Wesley in good stead when he reproved others. Once when dining with a friend, a preacher remarked on the abundance of food and asked Wesley what he thought of such a table as an example of self-denial. Wesley quietly suggested that the loaded table offered the perturbed preacher a most excellent opportunity to practice that virtue. At another time one of his preachers detected several rings on the hand of a daughter of his host. He called Wesley's attention and said, "What do you think of this, sir, for a Methodist hand?" The old man, whose distaste for jewelry was well known, smiled and answered, "The hand is very beautiful."

Such was the man who ruled the Methodists for fifty years. To them he was "Mr. Wesley," and happy was the household that could boast of entertaining him, and thrice happy was the Methodist who had the privilege of working with him, of being his "son in the gospel."

CHAPTER VIII

Interlude

In 1748, John Wesley was forty-five years old. For ten years he had labored unremittingly, traveling four or five thousand miles each year, mainly on horseback, and preaching incessantly. He had been busy extending the method of the Oxford Club, modified by his pietistic experience and sympathies, in the organization of thousands of converts scattered throughout the British Isles. At last Wesley paused to think of other things.

Since he left Georgia, Wesley had shown no signs of romantic interest in any woman. He had, of course, kept up a voluminous correspondence with many women who wrote him for counsel or showed appreciation of religious epistles from one of the best of English letter writers. Many details of society administration, as well as the oversight of the headquarters in London, Bristol, and Newcastle—often spoken of as Mr. Wesley's "houses" —required the services of women. But Wesley had entertained no thought of marrying. He had even published a tract recommending the celibate life as good for the soul. But in 1748 he changed his mind. His own account is that in a conference in London several of his brethren objected to his published views on marriage, and, he adds, "convinced me that a believer might marry without suffering loss in his soul."

Wesley's views on marriage were in part an inheritance from asceticism. He also supposed himself to have been convinced by the apostle Paul's practical observation that a married man has distractions which make it hard for him to serve the Lord with a single heart. The Pauline precept was italicized by Wesley's love affair with Sophia Hopkey, which showed the astonished Methodist how distracting such a passion can be. He was also influenced, characteristically enough, by his fear that marriage would abridge the funds available for his endless charities and would hinder his itinerant preaching. But all his objections were overcome by the arguments of his brethren assisted by his own experiences. In the latter category must be placed his acquaintance with Grace Murray.

Grace Murray was a sailor's widow and in 1748 was at the Orphan House in Newcastle, engaged in work with the societies there. She was born in Newcastle, her parents apparently having been small tradespeople. As a young woman Grace entered service in London and remained in a household in the metropolis until she married Murray. She had the orthodox Methodist experience, having heard Wesley before he went to America and having gone through many changes of hope and despair before her final conversion. In addition she was of mystical temperament but capable of practical and prolonged service, particularly in the peculiar work of the Methodist organization.

In August, 1748, following the conference in London when Wesley was convinced that he might lawfully marry, he fell ill at Newcastle and was nursed by Grace Murray. At this time he "observed her more narrowly than ever before, both as to her temper, sense, and behaviour." In truth Wesley never had time to observe any woman with reasonable "narrowness" except when he was ill. Sophia Hopkey had nursed him in Georgia, Grace Murray nursed him at Newcastle, and he was to have yet one more nurse. The result of Wesley's observations was that, when he had recovered a little, he spoke to Grace, "sliding into it" he knew not how. "If ever I marry," he said with noteworthy caution, "I think you will be the person." Later he spoke "more directly," and she seemed amazed. "This is too great a blessing for me," she cried; "I can't tell how to believe it. This is all I could have wished for under heaven—if I had dared to wish for it." Wesley naturally assumed that she had accepted him.

At her request he took her with him to visit the societies in Yorkshire and Derbyshire. Then he left her at Cheshire with one of his preachers, John Bennet. Did he remember that a year before Grace had nursed John Bennet through a serious illness?

Some time afterward Wesley received a letter from Bennet and another from Grace Murray asking his consent to their marriage. Wesley says that he was amazed, but he must have been busy with other matters, for he wrote a mild answer taking it for granted that they were already married. Instead of marrying Bennet, Grace Murray passed a distressed winter unable to choose between her two lovers. "One cannot excuse her behaviour all this time," observed her senior admirer, "doubtless she should have renounced one or the other. But those who know human nature will pity her much, at least as much as they will blame her."

In the spring Grace came to Bristol and explained to Wesley that she had not considered their contract binding because she could not think that what Wesley had proposed would ever come to pass. Reconciled, they went together to Ireland, spending several months visiting the societies. At this work Grace Murray was proficient. She met the women bands, visited the sick, prayed with the mourners, and in the meantime was an itinerant housekeeper for Wesley. At the end of the journey Wesley was more than ever in love, and on the return from Ireland they renewed their betrothal.

At Bristol one of the women in the society told Grace some idle gossip which caused her to write again to Bennet and renew her affair with him. In London a gossip advised her to leave off thinking of Wesley. The societies would make life too unpleasant, said this counselor; and the result would be misery for Wesley as well as his wife. When they arrived at Epworth, Wesley gave her up to Bennet on the assumption that she loved Bennet more. Then at Newcastle he accepted her again. At Berwick the distraught woman begged Wesley to marry her at once. He calmly replied that this could not be done, since it was necessary: " (1) To satisfy John Bennet; (2) to procure my Brother's consent; and (3) To send an Account of the reasons on which I proceeded, to every Helper and every Society in England, at the same time desiring their prayers." Grace Murray could only answer that she would not be willing to wait longer than one year, and Wesley reassured her that it might not take that long.

Having made clear to his fiancée his intention to abide by the rule of the Holy Club which forbade a member to marry without the consent of the others, Wesley settled down to write a forty-six-page account of the spiritual peregrinations of Grace Murray. Finishing that, in order "to form a clearer judgment of her real character," he "talked at large with all those who were disgusted at her, and inquired into their reasons for it." These reasons he found trivial enough. She was accused of having been so impudent as to ride into town alone with him, of having refused to lend her saddle, of having bought a Holland shift and a "Joseph" before she needed it, of being proud and insolent, of buying an apron worth ten shillings. These charges Wesley duly considered and absolved his intended bride on each count. He then turned to the first item on his program, the pacification of John Bennet. But while he was moving toward that, he was seized with a premonition of disaster. He was astonished to find himself beginning a letter to Grace with the lines:

"There is I know not what of sad presage,
  That tells me, we shall never meet again."

125

On the following Sunday words in the first lesson came "as a sword" to his heart: "Son of man, behold, I take away from thee the desire of thine eyes with a stroke." Eleven years before he had read these words in Savannah and had been "pierced through as with a sword." His love affairs coincided strangely with the calendar of lessons in the prayer book. This time also his forebodings were justified, for Charles was hastening to the rescue of the family name.

"The thought of marrying at all," so John interpreted his brother's attitude, "but especially of my marrying a servant and one so lowborn, appeared above measure shocking to him." On his way to Newcastle, Charles was informed that Grace Murray was really engaged to John Bennet. At Newcastle he was told that his brother was "beyond all sense and reason." Armed with such information, he burst in upon John, protesting that all the preachers would leave and the societies disperse if the leader "married so mean a woman." John placidly agreed to leave the matter to their mutual friend Vincent Perronet.

The better to answer Charles, who had declared that love had put out his brother's eyes, John sat down to write out a statement of his case. His paper, arrayed in thirty-two propositions, is irrefutable proof that, whatever else love had done for him, it had not affected his incurable passion for logic.

Wesley reviewed in his statement the reasons why he had held that a preacher, especially himself, should remain single. His theoretical objections had been removed by further study and the arguments of his brethren. His practical objections had been overcome in other ways. His belief that he could not afford a wife had held only until he had found that there were women in the world who were both able and willing to keep *him*. Moreover, his marriage would not add to his expense if he married one whom he supported already as his helper and who would be willing that their children (if any) should be educated at the school for preachers' children at Kingswood. Lastly, Grace Murray was the proper woman, for she would prove a helpmeet in his work. In support of this he arrayed her qualities in impressive paragraphs.

First, she was a good housekeeper. She was also a capable nurse, a qualification which his ill health at this period made doubly precious in his eyes. As a companion she had good sense and was "of a mild, sprightly, chearful, and yet serious temper." She was a tried and faithful friend, and—most important for *his* wife—she was possessed of "grace and gifts and fruit" as a laborer in the gospel of Christ.

On this last point Wesley was enthusiastic, not to say extravagant. His most fulsome praise was later crossed out of his manuscript, but its presence in the first draft testifies to the merits of Grace Murray as a Methodist. She would be willing and able to accompany him on his journeys. Her presence would defend him against "unholy desires and inordinate affections," which, he adds naïvely, "I never did entirely conquer for six months together" before meeting her. In addition to safeguarding her husband, she would safeguard others.

She would guard many from inordinate affection for me, to which they would be far less exposed, both because they would have far less hope of success, and because I should converse far more sparingly with them; perhaps not in private with any young women at all; at least not with any member of our own Societies.

As for the objections raised against the marriage, Wesley thought little of them. He cared not that his intended was not a gentlewoman; he did not hope to find a gentlewoman with the proper qualifications. Since Grace Murray had been his servant, he knew her all the better. At this time he thought he would marry no one who had not been with him some time. He was aware of what the gossips would say, that she had been his mistress before she was his wife. What if Grace Murray had traveled with him? He served notice on all that he would not marry any woman until he had proof that she both could and would travel with him. He was to remember this later.

So he marshaled his reasons, paraded them on his pages, marched them relentlessly to his conclusion: "(1) I have Scriptural reason to marry; (2) I know no person so proper as this."

Charles left the next morning, and while John went on about his preaching, having forebodings, dreaming of Grace Murray, examining his conscience to see if he were guilty of inordinate affection, and calmly committing the whole matter to God, Charles was bulldozing Grace Murray and persuading John Bennet. On November 5, 1749, someone came to Wesley and told him that Grace Murray and Bennet were married two days before. On the heels of this messenger came Charles to inform his brother that he had renounced all intercourse with him but such as he would have with a heathen man and a publican. But in a little while, amid the crying and entreaties of Whitefield and John Nelson, who were present, the two brothers fell on each other's necks. On the next day the bride and groom appeared, and Wesley learned the way in which Charles persuaded them to marriage. He forgave all, only adding, "Who can redress the wrong?" On his way to London, Wesley poured out his soul in thirty-one six-line stanzas. Later he quoted Lamentations: "Wherefore doth a living man complain, a man for the punishment of his sins?"

John Bennet soon left Wesley's connection and in later days was identified with his Calvinistic opponents. Years afterward Henry Moore went with Wesley, then an old man, to see Grace Bennet in London, where her son was preaching at a chapel in Moorfields. The meeting was soon over, and Wesley was never heard to mention her name again.

While the reader's mind is keyed to a minor note, the story of Wesley's love affairs may as well be concluded. Three years after John Bennet had married Grace Murray, the London papers announced that John Wesley had married a merchant's widow, one Mrs. Vazeille, then living in Threadneedle Street. They added various complimentary remarks, including the information that she had a jointure of ten thousand pounds.

Two weeks before his marriage John told Charles of his intention, but took care this time not to mention the lady's name. Charles, who had married four months after breaking up his brother's affair with Grace Murray, reacted according to formula:

> I was thunderstruck, and could only answer he had given me the first blow, and his marriage would come like the *coup de grâce*. Trusty Ned Perronet followed, and told me the person was Mrs. Vazeille—one of whom I never had the least suspicion. I refused his company to the chapel, and retired to mourn with my faithful Sally. Groaned all the day, and several following ones, under my own and the people's burden. I could eat no pleasant food, nor preach, nor rest either by night or by day.

But remembering perhaps the estrangement which almost resulted from his meddling in the Grace Murray affair, Charles this time attempted no interference. Crossing London Bridge on Saturday, February 10, 1751, John had fallen and struck his ankle against a stone. He preached that day, but as the sprain grew worse, he was removed to the home of Mrs. Vazeille. He spent the remainder of the week there, "partly in prayer, reading, and conversation, partly in writing an *Hebrew Grammar* and *Lessons for Children*." On the Monday following he was married.

Wesley had preached on Sunday, the day before his marriage; he likewise preached on Tuesday, the day after his marriage, although he was compelled to preach kneeling on account of his injury. Two weeks later he set out for Bristol, leaving his wife behind him. After returning to London for a few days, he started for the north. A month after his wedding he wrote in his *Journal*, perhaps with an eye on Charles, who had settled down after his happy marriage: "I cannot understand how a Methodist preacher can answer it to God, to preach one sermon or travel one day less, in a married than in a single state. In this respect surely 'it remaineth that they who have wives be as though they had none.'"

The newly wedded pair started off none too well. Wesley, having been the first to break the old rule of the Holy Club that none should marry without counseling with the others, felt called upon to explain his action to his brethren. Charles gives a terse account of his brother's apology, at which, he says, the preachers "hid their faces." The substance of John's remarks was:

That in Oxford [where he had been just before he announced to Charles his intention of marrying] he had an independent fellowship, was universally honoured, but left all for the people's sake; returned to town, took up his cross, and married; that at Oxford he had no more thought of a woman than for any other being; that he married to break down the prejudice about the world and him.

Charles adds that "his easily-won lady sat open-eyed." No wonder! The point of John's apology seems to have been that while at Oxford on a visit he had been tempted to resume his residence there, as he might under his fellowship. But for the sake of his work he had determined to continue and had decided that he ought to marry for the good of the cause. Marriage involved the resignation of his fellowship and put out of his way all possibility of return to the easy life of Oxford. But what an explanation for a bride, to be informed that two weeks before marriage her husband had never thought of such a thing, and that he had married her "to break down the prejudice about the world and him." The trouble had begun.

INTERLUDE

A few weeks after the wedding Wesley wrote his wife, adding an affectionate postscript to the effect that, if letters came addressed to "the Rev. Mr. Wesley," she was to open them. His lady did as she was told, and the amount of her husband's correspondence with other ladies throughout the United Kingdom began to dawn upon her. She at once objected to his correspondence with Sarah Ryan, the housekeeper at Bristol, who may at that time have been regenerate, but who had a past, which included three living husbands. Wesley refused to discontinue this correspondence.

Another item in the sum of their marital unhappiness was the failure of Mrs. Wesley to make a model traveling companion for her husband. This had been one of his first requirements for a wife and one of Grace Murray's excellences. The plight of a merchant's middle-aged widow, used to the peace of Threadneedle Street, in attempting to keep up with the most itinerant man in the British Isles may be glimpsed from the following incidents duly set down in the *Journal*:

While I was preaching at West Street [London] in the afternoon [the date was March 15, 1752] there was one of the most violent storms I ever remember. In the midst of the sermon great part of a house opposite to the chapel was blown down. We heard a huge noise, but knew not the cause; so much the more did God speak to our hearts; and great was the rejoicing of many in the confidence of His protection. Between four and five I took horse, with my wife and [step-] daughter. The tiles were rattling from the houses on both sides; but they hurt not us. We reached Hayes about seven in the evening, and Oxford the next day.

The next month he was mobbed in Hull. While he preached, clods and stones flew about on every side; and when he had finished, he found that his coachman had driven off.

We were at a loss till a gentlewoman invited my wife and me to come into her coach. She brought some inconveniences on herself thereby, not only as there were nine of us in the coach, three on each side, and three in the middle, but also as the mob closely attended us, throwing in at the windows (which we did not think it prudent to shut) whatever came next to hand. But a large gentlewoman who sat in my lap screened me, so that nothing came near me.

His wife grumbled at such traveling, as one would expect; and Wesley, naturally enough, resented her grumbling at a manner of life which had been his meat and drink for nearly twenty years. Of a journey which he made *without* his wife, he wrote:

In my present journey, I leap as broken from chains. I am content with whatever entertainment I meet with, and my companions are always in good humour, "because they are with me." This must be the spirit of all who take journeys with me. If a dinner ill dressed, or a hard bed, a poor room, a shower of rain, or a dusty road, will put them out of humour, it lays a burthen upon me greater than all the rest put together. By the grace of God, I never fret; I repine at nothing; I am discontented with nothing. And to hear persons at my ear fretting and murmuring at every thing is like tearing the flesh off my bones.

No one will wonder that a marriage between Wesley and Mrs. Vazeille did not succeed; one wonders only that anyone thought that it would. Wesley cannot be excused from blame. In the first place he was too old to marry, and in the second he lacked every requirement for a good husband. Southey may be right in saying that Mrs. Wesley deserves to be placed along with Xanthippe and Job's spouse as one of the three bad wives, but John Wesley deserves the place which someone has given him as one of the world's worst husbands.

For her part Mrs. Wesley was insanely jealous and capable of almost any meanness. She stole her husband's letters, even interpolating them with passages of questionable import, turning these mangled copies over to the public prints. At least once she attacked her distinguished husband with physical violence. Altogether it is a pitiable story.

In a long letter to his wife Wesley reviewed, with the inevitable numbered paragraphs, the story of his domestic shipwreck. He did not expect to be able to recall everything, he wrote, since he did not have his notes and his mind was "not very retentive of evil." Before his marriage he had seen that Mrs. Vazeille was "a well bred woman of great address and a middling understanding." Then one morning after their marriage he had found her "all thunder and lightning." To soften her temper, he had tried everything, argument—sometimes he "reasoned at large" with her—persuasions, silence. Nothing was of any effect; "one might as well attempt to convince or persuade the north wind." She had quarreled with his brother. She had been jealous of Mrs. Lefevre, "a dove-like woman," with whom he would have been glad to converse "frequently and largely." She had objected to the wife of his friend Ebenezer Blackwell. She broke into his cabinet, demanded to know every place he went and every person he saw there, and did not scruple to accuse him of adultery. At last he revolted.

"Perceiving you still rose in your demands, I resolved to break this at once, and to shew you I would be my own master, and go where I pleased without asking any one's leave." "You have wronged me much," he continued, "but not beyond forgiveness." Significant of his sentiments is the fact that his closing words were repeated in more than one letter to her:

I love you still, and am as clear from all other women as the day I was born. At length know *me* and know *yourself*. Your enemy I cannot be. But let me be your friend: suspect me no more: asperse me no more: provoke me no more. Do not any longer contend for mastery: for power, money, or praise. Be content to be a private insignificant person, known and loved by God and me. Attempt no more to abridge me of the liberty which I claim by God and man. Leave me to be governed by God and my own conscience:

Then shall I govern *you* with gentle sway, and shew that I do indeed love you, even as Christ the Church.

In the first weeks of 1771 Mrs. Wesley left her husband, whose *Journal* note on the event was nothing if not restrained: *"Non eam reliqui; non dimisi; non revocabo."* [1] There were temporary reconciliations after that, but no permanent one. On October 8, 1781, Mrs. Wesley died, at the age of seventy-one, after having for thirty years been a constant thorn in the side of the husband, who did not hear of her death until several days after she was buried.

[1] "I did not leave her; I did not send her away; I shall not call her back."

CHAPTER IX

On Several Occasions

THERE WERE other matters than affairs of the heart to claim Wesley's attention during the ten years after 1750. He moved among people stirred first by the fears that preceded and then by the suspense that followed the beginning of the Seven Years' War; he spoke to crowds excited by news of the fall of Louisburg, the battle of Minden, the attack on Quebec. Among the Methodists themselves there had arisen differences which taxed the skill and patience of their leader. Yet at no other time during his long life do Wesley's *Journal* and letters reflect more excursions into curious bypaths or more evidence of his incurable pragmatism.

On February 8, 1750, London was rocked by earthquake shocks. A second disturbance a month later roused the city almost to frenzy. A fanatic prophesied that on April 4 another earthquake would destroy half of London. The ensuing excitement was not cooled by sober warnings given out by those who seized the occasion to exhort the wicked. Charles Wesley preached a sermon on "The Cause and Cure of Earthquakes" and followed this by a pamphlet of hymns suitable for such calamities. Charles was at one with his brother in considering earthquakes as the instruments of God for punishing sin, for John was publicly thankful that the Lord had so lightly warned the people by the first shocks. In this opinion the Bishop of London concurred. His Lordship issued a pamphlet, of which sixty thousand were sold, pointing out the wickedness of the people and the possibility of grave judgments coming upon them.

During the three days preceding the fourth of April, the day set apart for the holocaust by the crazy prophet, 730 coaches were counted passing Hyde Park Corner carrying families to the open country. On the night of April 3 every open space in London was filled with people awaiting the end of the world. Many women wore specially prepared gowns, which Horace Walpole called "earthquake gowns." The occasion was made for Whitefield, and at midnight in Hyde Park he lifted up his voice in pitch darkness and exhorted shivering multitudes concerning wrath and judgment to come.

The ridicule which sheepish refugees poured out upon Bishop Sherlock after the first fright was over did not change Wesley's mind as to earthquakes. After the great Lisbon disaster in 1755 he issued a tract *Serious Thoughts on the Earthquake at Lisbon,* in which he insisted that irrespective of natural causes earthquakes are used as a means of divine justice. He added that, if the earthquake did not function, Halley's comet was expected in 1758 and might wreck the world.

In 1753 Wesley was often ill, but he continued to work. On October 22 he rode to Canterbury, although he was "extremely sick." All through the week he complained of sickness. He would have taken some rhubarb, but "had no time, having classes to meet from morning to night." The entry for Thursday, November 8, is:

In the night my disorder returned more violent than it had been since I left Cornwall. I should have taken some ipecacuanha in the morning, but had no time to spare, my business being fixed for every hour, till four in the afternoon; and by that time all my complaints were gone, so that I needed only a little food and rest.

His cough and fever increasing, Wesley thought best to write his epitaph "to prevent vile panegyric." Accordingly he composed the following inscription:

Here lieth the Body
of
JOHN WESLEY

A Brand Plucked Out of the Burning:
Who Died of a Consumption in the Fifty-First Year of His Age,
Not leaving, After His Debts are Paid,
Ten Pounds Behind Him:
Praying,
God be Merciful to Me, an Unprofitable Servant!

He ordered that this, if any, inscription should be placed on his tombstone.

In Charles's *Journal* the phrase "a brand plucked out of the burning" was amended by the words "not once only."

On January 3, 1754, Wesley arrived at Clifton, a suburb of Bristol, to take the cure at the Hot Well. Local tradition in Bristol has it that this was the beginning of the ruin of the Hot Well, for such notoriety came to Clifton as the result of the evangelist's visit and apparent benefit from the cure that the place was crowded with visitors. The overjoyed proprietors of the hot wells raised their prices so much that, when the first wave of popularity was over, the patronage dropped off, never to return.

On December 23, 1755, the Tory evangelist happened to be in the robing room which adjoined the House of Lords when the king, George II, put on his robes.

His brow was much furrowed with age [commented Wesley], and quite clouded with care. And is this all the world can give even to a king? All the grandeur it can afford? A blanket of ermine round his shoulders, so heavy and cumbersome he can scarce move under it! A huge heap of borrowed hair, with a few plates of gold and glittering stones upon his head! Alas, what a bauble is human greatness! And even this will not endure. Cover the head with ever so much hair and gold, yet—

> *Scit te Proserpina canum;*
> *Personam capiti detrahet illa tuo.*[1]

February 6 was a fast day, appointed because of a threatened French invasion. Wesley noted the words which were used in Jewish synagogues on that day:

Incline the heart of our Sovereign Lord King George, as well as the hearts of his lords and counsellors, to use us kindly, and all our brethren, the children of Israel, that in his days and in our days we may see the restoration of Judah, and that Israel may dwell in safety, and the Redeemer may come to Zion. May it be Thy will!

Wesley's most extended record during the fifties is of his visits to Ireland, but he was also in Scotland and Wales, and his English work included Cornwall and Yorkshire as well as his established headquarters in Bristol and London. Everywhere he had time to visit old buildings, explore natural wonders, inquire about strange occurrences and historic events, and compare the scenery and customs with those he had met elsewhere. To read his *Journal* is to pass in review the eighteenth century in the two kingdoms.

In Scotland, Wesley was amazed at the difference between conditions and the English report of them. In April, 1753, he stuck in a quagmire in the middle of the highroad on the way to Glasgow; but he could excuse this, "for the road all along, for near fifty miles after, was such as I never saw any natural road either in England or Ireland: nay, far better, notwith-

---

[1] "Proserpine knows you to be white-haired; she will strip off the mask from your head."

standing the continued rain, than the turnpike road between London and Canterbury."

Dumfries was

a clean, well-built town, having two of the most elegant churches (one at each end of the town) that I have seen. . . . What miserable accounts pass current in England of the inns in Scotland! Yet here, as well as wherever we called in our whole journey, we had not only everything we wanted, but everything readily and in good order, and as clean as I ever desire.

At Glasgow, Wesley visited the university, which he thought not larger or handsomer than Lincoln College. "The habit of the students gave me surprise. They wear scarlet gowns, reaching only to their knees. Most I saw were very dirty, some very ragged, and all of very coarse cloth."

At Alnwick, Wesley happened on the day when apprentices were made free of the corporation after completion of their time.

Sixteen or seventeen, we were informed, were to receive their freedom this day; and, in order thereto (such is the unparalleled wisdom of the present corporation, as well as of their forefathers), to walk through a great bog (purposely preserved for the occasion, otherwise it might have been drained long ago), which takes up some of them to the neck, and many of them to the breast.

Four years later Wesley was again in western Scotland. This time he went to the new library at the college in Glasgow and saw the collection of pictures. He walked through the old cathedral, which he thought more lofty than Canterbury. From the steeple he viewed the country: "A more fruitful and better cultivated plain is scarce to be seen in England. Indeed, nothing is wanting but more trade (which would naturally bring more people) to make a great part of Scotland no way inferior to the best counties in England."

Wesley thought that Edinburgh's main street (he spoke, of course, of the Old Town) was finer than anything in England. It was broad and finely paved and had

lofty houses on either hand (many of them seven or eight stories high). . . . But how can it be suffered that all manner of filth should still be thrown even into this street continually? Where are the magistracy, the gentry, the nobility of the land? . . . How long shall the capital city of Scotland, yea, and the chief street of it, stink worse than a common sewer?

In Holyrood Palace, Wesley was struck by the picture of Mary Queen of Scots. "It is scarce possible for any who looks at this to think her such a monster as some have painted her, nor indeed for any who considers the circumstances of her death, equal to that of an ancient martyr." In 1768 Wesley read a work dealing with the charges usually brought against Mary Stuart and was convinced, if he needed convincing, that Mary was innocent. To the objection that the character of Mary was generally called in question, he answered that the stories were circulated by Queen Elizabeth's orders. " 'But what, then, was Queen Elizabeth?' As just and merciful as Nero, and as good a Christian as Mahomet."

Various matters relative to conditions in Ireland adorn the Irish journals. He was in Castlebar on the western coast on the occasion of a "remarkable trial."

A Swedish ship, being leaky, put into one of our harbours. The Irish, according to custom, ran to plunder her. A neighboring gentleman hindered them, and, for so doing, demanded a fourth part of the cargo: and this, they said, the law allows! But where, meantime, is the law of God?

At Lurgan, in the north of Ireland, Wesley talked with a Mr. Miller, "the contriver of that statue which was in Lurgan

when I was there before." Wesley does not say that he ever saw
the machine, but he describes it:

It was the figure of an old man standing in a case, with a curtain
drawn before him, over against a clock which stood on the other
side of the room. Every time the clock struck he opened the door
with one hand, drew back the curtain with the other, turned his head
as if looking round on the company, and then said, with a clear, loud,
articulate voice: "Past one, two, three," and so on. But so many
came to see this (the like of which all allowed was not to be seen
in Europe) that Mr. Miller was in danger of being ruined, not
having time to attend his own business; so, as none offered to purchase it or to reward him for his pains, he took the whole machine
in pieces; nor has he any thought of ever making anything of the
kind again.[1]

On the occasion of a later visit, in 1773, Miller, who seems to
have been a gentleman of imagination, soberly assured Wesley
that he intended, "if he had life and health, to make two, which
would not only speak, but sing hymns alternately with an
articulate voice; that he had made a trial, and it answered well."
He prudently declined to say when it would be finished, as he
had other business and could only give his leisure time to the
work. Wesley did not proffer financial help, but observed,
"How amazing is it that no man of fortune enables him to give
all his time to the work!"

Such miscellaneous activities did not preclude from Wesley's
mind his one great problem in these years, a question which
had been asked much earlier and which was to be with him to
the end. Wesley had organized religious societies of such character that their relation to the established church was becoming
more and more difficult, and his own loyalty both to the
Establishment and to his societies created a dilemma.

---

[1] Miller was a "respectable woolen draper," *Methodist Magazine*, 1827, p.
801; but I have no further information about his supposed invention.

The Methodist societies were organized and controlled by the Wesleys, clergymen of the Church of England; and the majority of the members of these societies were at least nominal communicants of that church. But the opposition of bishops and clergy had early driven the Methodists into irregular practices, field preaching, the use of lay preachers, building of chapels. Many times Methodists were repelled from the sacraments, and often they themselves had scruples as to the lawfulness of receiving sacraments from unconverted priests. These conditions moved many of them to look longingly toward separation from the church.

Wesley's helpers were not always without ambition, and a connection with the church, which seemed very desirable to a fellow of Lincoln, held little attraction for men whom the church would not recognize. If Wesley could afford to endure the slights of his equals, his helpers could ill brook the same snubbing from social superiors. As dissenters, recognized nonconformists, they would at least have been free from galling attachment to the church.

The inherent difficulty of keeping Methodists faithful to the church appears more clearly as one looks closely at Wesley's societies. The sole condition of membership was a desire to flee from the wrath to come and to be saved from one's sins. True, Methodists were supposed to use the "means of grace," by which was meant church ordinances and services; but the astounding feature of this requirement, from a churchman's standpoint, was that dissenters might belong to the societies and satisfy the requirements of membership by attendance upon dissenting services. Wesley's principle was stated plainly:

We, by the grace of God, hold on our way; being ourselves still members of the Church of England, as we were from the beginning, but receiving all that love God in every Church, as our brother, and sister, and mother. And in order to their union with us, we require no unity in opinions, or in modes of worship, but barely that they "fear God and work righteousness," as was observed. . . . In what Church or congregation beside, throughout the Christian world, can members be admitted upon these terms, without any other conditions?

So concerned was he that his Methodists should have an outlook beyond the boundaries of the church that he took one evening a month during a certain period to read to the society "the accounts I received from time to time of the work which God is carrying on in the earth, both in our own and in other countries, not among us alone, but among those of various opinions and denominations." Wesley always contended that he allowed the greatest liberty of opinion within his societies, but one must interpret this broadly, remembering that the "evangelical" reading of Christianity was presupposed and that Wesley's allowance of difference of opinion did not mean permission for his preachers to disseminate doctrines which were considered erroneous. John Byrom, the poet, once took Wesley to task for turning out of his societies six men who, so Byrom contended, had been guilty only of reading the works of the mystic Jakob Böhme and of William Law. Wesley's answer was that the men were expelled for lying, that "he rejected them, not for reading the books, which was as indifferent as the colour of their hair, but if they would thrust their hair into other people's eyes, and trouble them with their notions—that was his reason." But essentially the societies rested upon a basis which could not but scandalize High Churchmen and tempt those who would separate from the Establishment. If dissenters could belong to the societies, why should not churchmen be free from the rule of unsympathetic clergymen and polemical bishops?

From the very first Wesley had valued his conscience above the bishops. In answer to a question from Charles as to what he should do if the bishops should forbid him preaching, John answered, as early as June 28, 1739: "God being my helper, I will obey Him still. And if I suffer for it, His will be done."

But Wesley was emphatic in insisting that the Methodists must remain with the church. In the first conference, 1744, one of the questions proposed was: "Do we separate from the Church?" The answer was: "We conceive not. We hold communion therewith for conscience' sake, by constant attending both the word preached and the sacraments administered therein." Another question of this first conference was: "Do you not entail a schism in the Church? that is, Is it not probable that your hearers, after your death, will be scattered into all sects and parties; or that they will form themselves into a distinct sect?" The answer is characteristic:

(1) We are persuaded the body of our hearers will even after our death remain in the Church, unless they be thrust out.

(2) We believe nothwithstanding, either that they will be thrust out, or that they will leaven the whole Church.

(3) We do, and will do, all we can to prevent those consequences which are supposed likely to happen after our death.

(4) But we cannot with a good conscience neglect the present opportunity of saving souls while we live, for fear of consequences which may possibly or probably happen after we are dead.

As the years went by, Charles was more and more perturbed, fearing that his brother would go too far toward dissent. "My chief concern upon earth," so he once told a conference of leaders, "was the prosperity of the Church of England; my next, that of the Methodists; my third, that of the preachers: that, if their interests should ever come into competition, I would give up the preachers for the good of the Methodists, and the Methodists for the good of the whole body of the Church of England." At another time he said that he remained with the Methodists, not so much to do good as to prevent evil. He wished to stand in the way of his brother's "violent counsellors." He feared that the tide would be too strong for him and "bear him away into the gulf of separation." Because of his anxious and officious interest for the church, Charles was disliked by many of the preachers, who saw in him the chief obstacle in the way of their plans for separation.

John Wesley's opinions underwent change through the years. From a High Churchman, believing in the divine right of episcopacy, he became a Low Churchman in his views on church and ministry. The development of his own doctrine as to church and orders need not be detailed here; the subject is a perennial one, particularly with the English Methodists, who find it necessary to defend the legitimacy of their church against Anglican assumptions. But John Wesley had been convinced that bishops and elders are of one and the same order, and that episcopacy, while convenient, is not prescribed of necessity in the New Testament. The consequence of this position is the belief that, if expedient, an elder can ordain as well as a bishop, and that obedience to the established order of the Church of England is not a necessity for salvation. Because John Wesley held this reformed view, Charles was convinced, as early as 1754, that his brother was almost ready for separation.

In the years 1755 and 1756 the question of separation was the burning issue. Charles thought all the preachers "in the north" unanimous for separation. But his brother stanchly denied this. "We have not one preacher," he wrote, "who either proposes, or desires, or designs (that I know) to separate from the church at all." He admitted some of the preachers held principles concerning ordination which he could not approve. But as to the future he was pragmatic. In answer to Charles's excited question as to what would be his response when the preachers in Ireland set up for themselves, as Charles was convinced they would shortly do, John Wesley returned the laconic answer, "When." To another clergyman who, like Charles, was worried about what might happen, Wesley responded that he, too, had spent much time in thinking about it, but could come to no decision. He wrote:

The steps I am *now* to take are plain. I see broad light shining upon them. But the other part of the prospect I cannot see: clouds and darkness rest upon it. Your general advice on this head—to follow my own conscience, without any regard to consequences, or prudence, so called—is unquestionably right; and it is a rule which I have closely followed for many years, and hope to follow to my life's end.

So Wesley went on calmly between two fires. On the one side Charles and his clerical friends besought him to take some step to insure his followers remaining with the church in case of their leader's death, which had been expected for several years. On the other side his preachers urged upon him greater concessions toward dissent. In this direction some of the preachers went so far as to administer the sacrament of the Lord's Supper without the authority of episcopal ordination. This they agreed to discontinue, but they maintained the lawfulness of the practice. Wesley in his course satisfied neither party.

Apparently only the leader of the Methodists could not or would not see the inevitable. He alone refused to face the real tendencies of his own movement. "It is a purely modern notion," writes a historian of the English Church, "that the Wesleyan movement ever was—or ever was intended to be, except by Wesley—a Church [of England] movement." The exception is significant. Only Wesley thought it possible to create a brotherhood which would transcend denominational differences; only Wesley refused to accept the obvious limitations of ecclesiastical Christianity.

In 1757 Charles Wesley ceased to travel as an itinerant preacher. He settled with his wife, formerly Sarah Gwynne, in

Bristol. Various reasons have been given for Charles's action. He continued with his brother in charge of the societies; he was as much a Methodist as he had ever been. His marriage may have had something to do with his decision. So thought one of his friends, Berridge, who contrasted Charles's condition with that of John Wesley and George Whitefield. "No trap so mischievous to the field preacher as wedlock," Berridge wrote to Lady Huntingdon. "Matrimony has quite maimed poor Charles, and might have spoiled John and George, if a wise Master had not graciously sent them a brace of ferrets."

Whatever the reason for Charles's withdrawal from the itinerancy, John Wesley was left the sole itinerant superintendent of the societies. In spite of his perplexities and his disappointment at his brother's retirement, he moved steadily about his work; and the decade ends with a characteristic blending of national and Methodist interests. In November, 1759, Wesley observed in London the General Thanksgiving appointed for the success of British arms at Quebec and Minden, the battles which won Canada and saved Hanover for the English Crown. The day was observed at the Methodist chapel near the Seven Dials with two sermons from John Wesley, who remarked that perhaps for the first time in the history of Europe the prayers for such a day included a petition for the enemies of England.

CHAPTER X

An Itinerant Mind

W<small>ESLEY'S</small> <small>PHYSICAL</small> activities were so stupendous that the casual reader of his biography may overlook his intense mental vigor. The restless activity which drove him to Georgia was unsatisfied with a score of years of travel, preaching, and administration. In this orderly opportunist, this evangelistic don, was a full measure of the adventuring spirit which put Sterne to trifling with new prose forms, set Watt to building steam engines, and sent Cook to the South Seas. Mentally as well as physically Wesley was an itinerant; the world was his parish. His *Journal* reflects this roving, curious mind. Theology, politics, literature, folklore, wonder tales, jostle one another in the crowded pages. His publications, pamphlets, letters to the newspapers, were on all subjects. A survey of his mental parish is a survey of the intellectual interests of the eighteenth century in England.

A glance at the index of his collected works finds such variety as this: "Remarks on Mr. H.'s Account of the Gentoo Religion in Hindostan"; "Thoughts upon Baron Montesquieu's 'Spirit of the Laws'"; "Thoughts on the Character and Writings of Mr. Prior"; "Thoughts on the Writings of Baron Swedenborg"; "Remarks on the Count De Buffon's 'Natural History'"; "Remarks upon Mr. Locke's 'Essay on Human Understanding'";

"Remarks on Mr. Bryant's 'Analysis of Ancient Mythology'";
"Thoughts upon Taste"; "Thoughts on the Power of Music";
"A Thought on the Manner of Educating Children"; "Thoughts
on Genius"; "Thoughts on Suicide"; "An Account of the Disturbance in my Father's House" (Old Jeffrey, the ghost);
"Directions concerning Pronunciation and Gesture." His
journals show him continually turning aside to examine some
natural wonder or archæological remains. At times he himself
tried curious experiments, as when he took a musician with
him and observed the effect of music upon the lions in the
Tower. His contemporaries wondered at his versatility. When
he took dinner with the Bishop of Exeter, in 1782, the guests
were astonished that the venerable Methodist had investigated
the question of Chatterton's authorship of the Rowley papers.

Samuel Wesley had hoped that his son would follow "critical
learning." Perhaps he dreamed that John would beget some
ponderous volumes such as his own *Dissertationes ad Librum
Jobi*. But Susannah Wesley better understood her son and recommended "practical divinity." Indeed, John's mind was not
that of a scholar, diligently searching for his facts and patiently
studying and comparing his findings. He himself has best described his own mental processes. In his *Journal*, on July 3, 1764,
he writes:

I was reflecting on an odd circumstance, which I cannot account
for. I never relish a tune at first hearing, not till I have almost
learned to sing it; and, as I learn it more perfectly, I gradually lose
my relish for it. I observe something similar in poetry; yea, in all
the objects of the imagination. I seldom relish verses at first hearing; till I have heard them over and over, they give me no pleasure;
and they give me next to none when I have heard them a few
times more, so as to be quite familiar. Just so a face or a picture,
which does not strike me at first, becomes more pleasing as I grow
more acquainted with it; but only to a certain point: for when
I am too much acquainted, it is no longer pleasing.

This is not the way of "critical learning," but it is the way of that type of mind to which everything new is a challenge to be followed until it is no longer new. Wesley had the mind of the traveler, the explorer; and like many explorers, he often believed as he wanted to believe.

Wesley scoffed at Goldsmith's uncritical belief in the existence of Bishop Pontoppidan's kraken and sea serpent, the one a mile across and the other raising himself out of the water higher than the mainmast of a man-of-war. But Wesley himself was always open to a good ghost story. The famous one which came from his father's house had doubtless helped to confirm him in his childhood belief, a belief reinforced by his uncritical assumptions concerning the Bible. Giving up belief in witchcraft, he said, was "in effect giving up the Bible." He could not but wonder at men denying "dogmatically" "what not only the whole world, heathen and Christian, believed in past ages, but thousands, learned as well as unlearned, firmly believe at this day." In the same way trivial happenings were attributed by him to direct intervention of God, to the scandal of sober churchmen and the later embarrassment of devout biographers. Wesley's explanations of this habit were ingenious if not convincing. He was once lost in the darkness and rain; he prayed for the rain to stop, or for a light, or for an honest guide. Presently he got all three. When accused of claiming this as a miracle, he denied vehemently; the incident was "but a signal instance of God's particular providence over all those who call upon him."

As a good Englishman, Wesley shared many of the robust prejudices of his day. While speaking against persecution and bravely denouncing the Lord Gordon riots, he nevertheless opposed the Toleration Act, which proposed to remove the disabilities of the Romanists. "I will not," he wrote, "use the sword against them, nor put it into their hands, lest they should use it against me; I wish them well, but I dare not trust them." In the same way he shared the feelings of his patriotic fellow countrymen concerning everything French. Having read Voltaire's *Henriade* he allowed him to be "a perfect master of the French language," but added:

By him I was more than ever convinced that the French is the poorest, meanest language in Europe; that it is no more comparable to the German or Spanish than a bag-pipe is to an organ; and that, with regard to poetry in particular, considering the incorrigible uncouthness of their measure, and their always writing in rhyme (to say nothing of their vile double rhymes, nay, and frequent false rhymes), it is as impossible to write a fine poem in French as to make fine music upon a jews'-harp.

Always Wesley's mind was directed by practical interests. A fact was something that could not be explained away, explain it as one might. Indeed, he would accept the most startling explanations if they seemed to justify the fact. In the preface to his *A Survey of the Wisdom of God in the Creation* he wrote:

It will be easily observed, that I endeavour throughout, not to account for things; but only to describe them. I undertake barely to set down what appears in nature; not the cause of those appearances. The facts lie within the reach of our senses and understanding; the causes are more remote. That things are so, we know with certainty; but why they are so, we know not.

This truly scientific statement is applicable to his central religious beliefs. He was convinced of the truth of the semimystical teachings of the Pietists only by the testimony of those who claimed to have experienced assurance of their personal touch with the Divine. During his active ministry he carefully gathered biographical accounts of religious experience, until by the time of his death he had amassed a unique body of such literature. These accounts were published from time to time, on the principle that such firsthand testimony is far better for all readers than works about religion. More than one book on the psychology of religion has been based upon this source material.

It would be untrue to say that Wesley developed his theology out of this data. When he became theological in thinking or writing, he was used to employing the categories of traditional Christian theology, choosing freely, it is true, and sometimes making strange dogmatic bedfellows to lie down together. But when he wrote for the man of the world or spoke to the ignorant, he was unfettered and used words that all men could understand. For this reason such writings as his *Appeal to Men of Reason and Religion* may be used today, while his *Standard Sermons* are perused only by Methodist preachers who are still compelled to read them, with the result that they often go forth believing Wesley a flogger of dead asses and his religion a matter of whereases and therefores. His true theological emphasis, as has been well said, was upon three things: moral idealism, certainty, and "his universal appeal to mankind to believe in God as Infinite Love."

As for his technical theological treatises and his theological controversies, are they not written in all the "lives" of Wesley? He who cares to wade through them will find much refreshment if his soul longs for dreary arguments on "Original Sin," "Predestination," and "Free Grace." But even in argument Wesley sometimes swerves with lightness or parries his opponent's thrust with grace. Against such opponents as the Rev. Augustus Toplady, author of the hymn "Rock of Ages" and of much scurrility and low abuse, Wesley retained his dignity; and the character of his tracts stands out against the personal slander of much of the theological controversy of the period. Yet Wesley's very self-restraint was better calculated to exasperate his opponents than much railing.

When Toplady wrote at length in favor of the doctrine of

predestination, Wesley summed up his opponent's belief with a terseness that put the reverend author beside himself with rage:

The sum of all is this: One in twenty (suppose) of mankind are elected; nineteen in twenty are reprobated. The elect shall be saved, do what they will; The reprobate shall be damned, do what they can. Reader, believe this, or be damned. Witness my hand. A—T—.

Toplady's friend Rowland Hill, editor of a "religious" paper called the *Review* abused Wesley shamefully. Wesley replied at length and at the end deplored Hill's manner. "How is it," asked Wesley, "that as soon as a man comes to the knowledge of the truth, it spoils his temper?" Hill, formerly an amiable man, was now "violent, impetuous, bitter of spirit! in a word, the author of the *Review!*" But Wesley did not always deal in soft answers. His opponents had been quick to see that, when Wesley reprinted Bunyan's *Holy War*, he left out that worthy's Calvinism. They immediately accused him of having "disemboweled" poor John Bunyan to make him look like Wesley. No, said Wesley, Bunyan was abridged to fit into the scheme of the publications in which he was included. "However," he retorted, "those that are fond of his bowels may put them in again, and swallow them as they would the trail of a woodcock."

To tell the truth, Wesley rather enjoyed a good controversy. He had learned to love it in a university where men learned by disputing. He thanked God that at Lincoln, as moderator in the disputations which were held there six times a week, he learned the "honest art" of arguing. And he observed with more truth than modesty: "At doing this, I bless God, I am expert; as those will find who attack me without rhyme or reason." Wesley answered his critics in good eighteenth-century fashion, paragraph by paragraph, stopping occasionally to criticize their use of a word or to raise an eyebrow at their constructions, and often ending with a word of advice as to the spirit and method best adapted to such debate. Altogether he was perhaps the most maddening, if not the ablest, of those who in that contentious age deluged the booksellers with inky divinity.

Wesley's literary taste was determined mainly by his youthful training and by his moral interests. As an Oxonian he had reveled in light literature, especially in plays. Such reading he later bemoaned as a sinful waste of time, but as he grew older, his catholic taste again prevailed. He was always a stern critic of any immoral tendencies in literature, but his reading was wider than the lesser minds of his helpers could understand. To his niece Sally he recommended a course of reading which included the *"Fairy Queen,* select parts of Shakespeare, Fairfax's or Hoole's *Godfrey of Bouillon, Paradise Lost,* the *Night Thoughts,* and Young's *Moral and Sacred Poems."*

Mention of Young recalls the popularity of the melancholy poets among the Methodists. Blair, Graves, and Young were quoted at great length, until a scoffer said that these poets little dreamed, when they wrote, that they were composing verses for the Methodists. In this, however, the Methodists shared the taste of the age. Wesley himself admired the classics and quoted Greek and Latin on all occasions, as did all the university men of his day; but he thought Goldsmith a fine writer, admired Dr. Johnson, and was impressed with Macpherson's *Fingal* when it was palmed off as an ancient northern saga. He read *Fingal* through twice and concluded it to be genuine and second only to Virgil and Homer.

Matthew Prior, a friend of Samuel Wesley the younger, was one for whom John Wesley had great esteem. He quoted him on many occasions and wrote a defense of his poetry. In this essay Wesley judged Prior superior to Pope in "natural understanding," believing that those lines which the poet polished carefully were not inferior to "anything that has been wrote either by Pope, or Dryden, or any English poet, except

Milton." His opinions fluctuated, it would seem; for nearly twenty years before, he had written:

I was myself once much fonder of Prior than Pope; as I did not then know that stiffness was a fault. But what in all Prior can equal for beauty of style some of the first lines that Pope ever published?

Wesley was particularly interested in history and did not confine himself to ecclesiastical lines. In his recommendations to his niece he included a rather heavy diet of historical writings: "You may begin with Rollin's *Ancient History*," he wrote the young lady, "and afterwards read in order the *Concise History of the Church*, Burnet's *History of the Reformation*, the *Concise History of England*, Clarendon's *History of the Rebellion*, Neal's *History of the Puritans*, his *History of New England*, and Robertson's *History of America*."

The concise histories mentioned in the letter were compiled by Wesley himself. As usual he objected to verbose works and therefore undertook to abridge and popularize Mosheim's *Ecclesiastical History* and to compile a history of England. This latter he took largely from Rapin, Goldsmith, and Smollett. Much of the material in histories, he contended, was of no more importance than news that a bird had dropped a feather on one of the "Pyrenæan Mountains." He desired, too, to accustom his readers to seeing the hand of God in history; and, one must add, he also desired to propagate his own ideas about certain historical characters. He adopted "revisionist" views concerning Richard III and Mary Queen of Scots, and hoped to do justice to "those greatly injured characters." His histories were not successful, and an early biographer cumbrously explains that "the too great confidence he had in the authority of his own assertions . . . in some degree indisposed him to enter into that detail of evidence from facts so highly necessary to establish a general principle in history and biography."

Wesley's delicate health in his youth and young manhood early directed his attention to medicine. The *Journal* records several severe illnesses, notably those in Bristol in 1741 and in London in 1753. But Wesley's interest in medicine went far beyond his own case. In almost all his journeys he prescribed for sick Methodists. This was in accord with tradition, as the example of Richard Baxter and the advice of George Herbert in the seventeenth century testify; but Wesley's interest naturally enough expressed itself in an evangelistic manner. What he himself believed to be worth while, he felt impelled to pass on to others.

His principal effort in this line was the publication of his *Primitive Physick; or, an Easy and Natural Method of Curing Most Diseases,* to which he prefixed the characteristic motto: *Homo sum; humani nihil a me alienum puto.* The first edition of this work was printed in 1747. The year that the author died, the twenty-third edition came from the press. At various times during these forty-three years it was revised and enlarged. This book Wesley commended to his congregations, advising the societies in Bristol, for example, that if they had any regard for their bodies or their childern, they should have a copy in every house.

Primitive Physick was an outgrowth of the dispensary which Wesley instituted in 1746. He explained:

For six or seven-and-twenty years, I had made anatomy and physic the diversion of my leisure hours; though I never properly studied them, unless for a few months when I was going to America, where I imagined I might be of some service to those who had no regular physician among them.

When he established his dispensary in London, Wesley employed an apothecary and an experienced surgeon, and resolved not to go out of his depth, "but to leave all difficult and com-

plicated cases to such physicians as the patients should choose."
But he did not usually think highly of physicians. Four months
after he opened the dispensary he wrote to Archbishop Secker
that for more than twenty years he had had numberless proofs
"that regular physicians do exceeding little good." An exception was made in the case of those whom he regarded as
honest as well as skillful, concerning whom he quoted Ben-
Sirach (Ecclesiasticus xxxviii. 1, 2) : "Honour the physician, for
God hath appointed him."

Wesley's medical knowledge and practice must be judged
in the light of his purpose and times. He was a confessed amateur and had the amateur's scorn of the professional. But he was
moved by the misery of people in the poorer sections of London
and in remote country districts, all suffering for lack of medical
care. To quote again from his letter to Archbishop Secker:

Now, ought I to have let one of these poor wretches perish, because I was not a regular physician? to have said, "I know what
will cure you; but I am not of the college; you must send for Dr.
Mead [the most distinguished and socially prominent physician of
the day]?" Before Dr. Mead had come in his chariot, the man might
have been in his coffin. And when the doctor was come, where was
his fee? What! he cannot live upon nothing! So, instead of an
orderly cure, the patient dies; and God requires his blood at my
hands.

Primitive Physick contains 725 prescriptions for 243 diseases.
Many of the remedies would startle a modern reader. One finds
such recommendations as this: for "a consumption"

take a *cowheel* from the tripe-house ready drest, two quarts of *new
milk,* two ounces of *hartshorn shavings,* two ounces of *isinglass,* a
quarter of a pound of *sugar-candy,* and a race of *Ginger.* Put all
these in a pot: and set them in an oven after the bread is drawn. Let
it continue there till the oven is near cold: and let the patient live
on this.

Most of his prescriptions, however, are simpler, as when for "Raging Madness" he advises, "Let him eat nothing but *apples* for a month."

The real merit of Wesley's medical advice is found not in his specific remedies, but in his attitude toward medicine. One can, indeed, hardly quarrel with his drugs, remembering that heterogeneous compounds of from twenty to seventy ingredients were not unknown to the apothecaries, and that the *London Pharmacopœia* of 1721, the official druggists' directions issued by the College of Physicians, contained as ingredients in certain formulas "dogs' excrement, earthworms, and moss from the human skull." In his preface Wesley inveighs against "compound medicines, consisting of so many ingredients that it was scarce possible for common people to know which it was that wrought the cure." He contended:

> The common method of compounding and decompounding medicines, can never be reconciled to common sense. Experience shows that one thing will cure most disorders, at least as well as twenty put together. Then why do you add the other nineteen? Only to swell the apothecary's bill; nay, possibly, on purpose to prolong the distemper, that the doctor and he may divide the spoil.

Physicians of the eighteenth century were given to seeking after "complete theoretical systems" in which mathematics, mechanics, even astronomy, played a part. Against these tendencies a few great names in the later seventeenth and early eighteenth centuries can be quoted. Thomas Sydenham (1624-89) was not a thoroughgoing empiric, but he set his face away from theoretical systems in the direction of a return to nature. In Holland, Hermann Boerhaave (1668-1738) became the founder of a school of medicine which followed the more or less empirical methods of Sydenham. Lesser names could be mentioned, two of whom are referred to by Wesley. The subject is important here for one reason: an amateur and popularizer in any field is to be judged largely by the authorities whom he follows. A quotation from Wesley's preface will make clear his own position:

> Yet there have not been wanting, from time to time, some lovers of mankind who have endeavoured (even contrary to their own interest) to reduce physic to its ancient standard; who have laboured to explode out of it all the hypotheses, and fine spun theories, and to make it a plain intelligible thing, such as it was in the beginning, having no more mystery in it than this, "Such a medicine removes such a pain." . . .
> Even in the last age there was something of this kind done, particularly by the great and good Dr. Sydenham; and in the present by his pupil Dr. Dover, who has pointed out simple medicines for many diseases. And some such may be found in the writings of the learned and ingenious Dr. Cheyne.

Wesley's authorities were good, although he, as many popularizers, assumed a simplicity which does not exist and reduced medicine to an empiric science, indeed: "such a medicine removes such a pain." His guides were men who were moving slowly in the direction which medicine was to take in the century of Lister and Pasteur.

The last name mentioned in the quotation above is that of George Cheyne, of Bath, two of whose books influenced Wesley's health habits in no small degree. Wesley wrote to his mother in 1724 concerning Cheyne's *Book of Health and Long Life* in which health was referred mainly to temperance and exercise. In the same year Wesley read Cheyne's *Natural Method of Curing Disease* and admired it, although he doubted that it would influence an epicure, since Cheyne talked "against good eating and drinking." From Cheyne, Wesley abstracted most of his rules for health to which he gave first place in *Primitive Physick*. These rules recommend cleanliness of person and surroundings, light and careful eating, water-drinking, avoidance of liquors both strong and malt—"except clear small beer, of a due age"—disuse of coffee and tea by nervous persons, walking as the best exercise, few clothes, cold bathing, avoidance of passions, and—the love of God. His rules of health possibly neutralized some of his remedies.

In the preface to the 1760 edition of *Primitive Physick*, Wesley recommended electricity as "the nearest an universal medicine, of any yet known in the world." This remedy appears throughout later editions. Even for "Old Age," along with the use of tar-water [1] and "decoction of nettles," he advised: "Be electrified daily." The mention of electricity introduces other scientific fields into which Wesley entered as intrepidly as into that of medicine.

As early as 1747 Wesley went to see "the electrical experiments" and reported his astonishment at seeing a flame issue from his finger, "real flame, such as sets fire to spirits of wine." At this time "electrical machines" were being carried over England for the purpose of demonstrating to the curious the method of generating and storing electricity which had become famous as the result of the experiments of Dutch scholars at Leiden. Popular interest was reflected in articles and letters which appeared in the public prints, and possible medicinal use of the new discovery was early debated. A letter in the *Gentleman's Magazine* for May, 1747, tells of a reported cure of a rheumatic pain by electrification and adds, "Who knows what farther experiments and discoveries such an incident may lead to?" The letter is signed "J. W." Wesley himself followed Benjamin Franklin's publications on electricity with much interest. These were originally sent to London in letters to Peter Collinson, an American merchant and member of the Royal Society; but the Society did not think them worthy of inclusion in their published transactions. They were at last published in England by Cave, editor of the *Gentleman's Magazine*.

[1] Tar-water was Bishop Berkeley's panacea which he advocated in *Philosophical Reflexions and Inquiries Concerning the Virtues of Tar-Water,* published in 1744.

Wesley's interests were primarily practical. He was curious and always willing to read anyone's theory, but his reply to a question in one of his conferences defines the scope of his major enthusiasm: "Why did you meddle with electricity? For the same reason as I published the *Primitive Physick*—to do as much good as I can."

In 1756 Wesley set up an electrical machine, not for experiment but for medical purposes. Two or three years afterward the patients were so numerous that they were divided, and "part were electrified in Southwark, part at the Foundery, others near St. Paul's, and the rest near the Seven Dials." In 1760 he published *"The Desideratum; or, Electricity Made Plain and Useful. By a Lover of Mankind and of Common Sense."* Half of this work was taken up with accounts of experiments and theories concerning electricity, half with accounts of cases of ailments relieved by application of the newly discovered power. His work was taken, he said, from what had been published on the subject by "Mr. Franklin, Mr. Hoadly, Mr. Wilson, Watson, Lovett, Freke, Martin, Watkins, and in the Monthly Magazines." For the speculative part he was chiefly indebted to Franklin, and for the practical part, to Lovett, although he did not subscribe to everything that they said.

For the understanding of Wesley's general scientific position, one must turn primarily to *A Survey of the Wisdom of God in the Creation: or, A Compendium of Natural Philosophy.* This was first published in 1763 in two volumes. In 1770 a new edition was published in three volumes, while the third edition, published in 1777, contained five volumes.

The object of this work was stated in the preface to the first edition:

I have long desired to see such a compendium of natural philosophy, as was, (1) Not too diffuse, not expressed in many words. . . .

(2) Not maimed or imperfect; but containing the heads of whatever (after all our discoveries) is known with any degree of certainty, either with regard to the earth or heavens. And this I wanted to see, (3) In the plainest dress; simply and nakedly expressed, in the most clear, easy, and intelligible manner, that the nature of the things would allow; particularly, free from all the jargon of mathematics, which is mere Heathen Greek to common readers. At the same time, I wished to see this short, full, plain account of the visible creation directed to its right end: not barely to entertain an idle, barren curiosity; but to display the invisible things of God, his power, wisdom, and goodness.

Such a treatise Wesley had been unable to find in English and had therefore turned to foreign sources. He found what he wanted in the Latin work of Johann Franz Buddeus (1667-1729). Buddeus was professor of philosophy in Jena after 1705, a celebrated theologian of his day who wrote in several fields. Wesley took his work, but

found occasion to retrench, enlarge, or alter every chapter, and almost every section. . . . So that [he added] it is now, I believe, not only pure, containing nothing false or uncertain; but as full as any tract can be expected to be, which is comprised in so narrow a compass: and, likewise plain, clear, and intelligible to one of a tolerable understanding.

In the preface to his third edition Wesley wrote that he had finished his revision before he saw Oliver Goldsmith's *History of the Earth and Animated Nature.* "I had not read over the first volume of this," he continued, "when I almost repented of having wrote any thing on the head." His opinion of Goldsmith was high: "He was a person of strong judgment, of a lively imagination, and a master of language, both of the beauty and strength of the English tongue."

Nevertheless, Wesley objected to many things in Goldsmith's book. The author spent too much time on animals commonly known, which can be "at least, useful only to the booksellers, by swelling the bulk, and consequently the price of his book." The work was too large and expensive. Wesley thought his own sources more abundant than Goldsmith's, but he found the latter's accounts sometimes more accurate than his own; so he had substituted passages from Goldsmith, only abbreviating as space demanded. Besides, Wesley inserted "several of his [Goldsmith's] beautiful remarks, such as directly tended to illustrate that great truth—'O Lord, how manifold are thy works! In wisdom hast thou made them all.' "

In the fourth volume of the third edition Wesley added an abridgment of Charles Bonnets *Contemplation of Nature,* which had appeared in Amsterdam in 1764 and in England in translation in 1766. In the fifth volume were extracts from *Inquiry into the Origin of the Discoveries Attributed to the Moderns,* by Deutens. An appendix contained a study of the human understanding after Peter Browne, Bishop of Cork.

The *Compendium* was designed to cover all branches of natural science, and the headings of the main sections show that this purpose was carried out. The various books are entitled: "Of Man," "Of Brutes," "Of Plants," and "Of Natural Bodies," to which were added abridgments of the dissertations referred to above. The introduction surveys the progress of science, referring especially to new discoveries and inventions. Among these are listed the discovery in medicine of the circulation of the blood, of the lacteal veins, of the thoracic duct, and of the possibility of transfusion of blood. In the organic world the discovery of variations of the lodestone is mentioned, along with the invention or development of the microscope, barometer, thermometer, air pump, diving bell, the telescope, and a "diving-machine"—"a kind of boat, which is so contrived as to be navigated under water." Along with these discoveries and inventions, which represent very fairly the major scientific accomplishments of Wesley's day, there are set down as true certain of the current misconceptions of his time. He records, for example, the contemporary doctrine of spontaneous generation, a theory which held the field until the early nineteenth century proved the opposing theorem, that all life comes from life. He also explained the revolution of the earth as being caused by the action of the sun's rays in striking the surface of the earth obliquely, as the wind strikes the sails of a windmill.

This is only to say that Wesley made no original contribution to science. But he faithfully recorded the opinions of those whom he considered the best guides, and it is to his credit that his judgment in general has been justified by history. Needless to say, the *Compendium* is of no value now; for, as always, Wesley was writing for his own audience and for a very practical purpose. He interjected remarks of his own, sometimes with his tongue in his cheek and sometimes in his earnestness forgetting his humor. He admired the adaptability of nature. "Nor is it an uncommon thing to see the favorite lapdog fed out of the same bowl of milk, which is prepared for the heir of a wealthy family, but which nature originally designed to nourish a calf." Or again, he noticed a story of a man in Bristol who was reputed to chew the cud. "What a mercy is it," exclaimed Wesley, "that we have not more such instances! For how much of our precious time would it consume!"

A section of the *Compendium* which has been much quoted in recent years is that in which Wesley abridged Bonnet's exposition of the doctrine of the universal chain of being—*scala naturæ*. This passage is often quoted as an evidence that Wesley, thirty-two years before Darwin's birth, had foreshadowed the evolutionary theory of the development of life. On the other hand, one writer, who really has some understanding of the true meaning of the "chain of being," cites this as an "anti-evolutionary" doctrine, remarking, somewhat naïvely, that it is doubtful if Wesley had ever heard of the theory of evolution. The notoriety which has been given these quotations makes it worth while to quote more of the section than is ordinarily given and to point out the real significance of the statements included from Bonnet.

Wesley's own statement of the doctrine of *scala naturæ* is as follows:

The whole progress of nature is so gradual, that the entire chasm from a plant to man, is filled up with divers kinds of creatures, rising one above another, by so gentle an ascent, that the transitions from one species to another, are almost insensible. And the intermediate space is so well husbanded, that there is scarce a degree of perfection which does not appear in some.

Bonnet explained the idea more at length:

Between the lowest and highest degrees of corporeal and spiritual perfection, there is an almost infinite number of intermediate degrees. The result of these degrees composes the universal chain. This unites all beings, connects all worlds, comprehends all the spheres. One Sole Being is out of this chain, and that is He that made it.

There are no sudden changes in nature; all is gradual, and elegantly varied. There is no being which has not either above or beneath it some that resemble it in certain characters, and differ from it in others.

Among these characters which distinguished beings, we discover some that are more or less general. Whence we derive our distributions into classes, genera, and species. But there are always between two classes, and two like genera, mean productions, which seem not to belong more to one than to the other, but to connect them both.

The polypus links the vegetable to the animal. The flying squirrel unites the birds to the quadruped. The ape bears affinity to the quadruped and the man.

In another place, discussing the progression of beings from the lowest up through the highest animals to man, there is the often quoted passage:

By what degrees does nature raise herself up to man? How will she rectify this head that is always inclined towards the earth? How change these paws into flexible arms? What method will she make use of to transform these crooked feet into supple and skilful hands? Or how will she widen and extend this contracted stomach? In what manner will she place the breasts, and give them a roundness suitable to them?

The ape is this rough draught of man: this rude sketch, an imperfect representation, which nevertheless bears a resemblance to him, and is the last creature that serves to display the admirable progression of the works of God.

This theory of a universal chain of being, so well stated in Bonnet's work, was enunciated chiefly by Bonnet in Geneva and by the Count de Buffon and Lamarck in France. The last named later rejected the doctrine. As to this theory's relations to the later doctrine of evolution, three points must be kept in mind. The observations upon which the chain-of-being theory was based were superficial. It was the naturalist Cuvier who later proposed grouping animals on the basis of comparative anatomy. In the second place, family relations and groupings of species were largely ignored, on the presumption that all life was connected in linear fashion from the simplest to the most complicated forms. Finally, this theory held rigidly to the immutability of species; there was no thought of the evolution of one species from another.

There is, however, no point in speaking of *scala naturæ* as an antievolutionary theory. The theory of evolution, as we know it, was simply nonexistent in Wesley's day; and the chain-of-being conception was one of the many preliminary stages of scientific theory on the way to the nineteenth century's favorite hypothesis. In his own day Wesley adopted and set forth the theory which seemed to him the most brilliant generalization, which seemed to him most to glorify God. If there is an endless chain of being, he asked, does it not include supernatural beings as well as natural ones? He quoted with approval John Locke's argument that there are doubtless more species above us than below us. The conception of a scale of being fitted into his scheme because it served the end for which he wrote his book, "to display the invisible things of God, his Power, Wisdom and Goodness." As to his possible reactions to the theory of evolution, a theory which had not been promulgated in his day, this question must be left to the sons of the prophets. All that any sober reader of Wesley's *Compendium* can say is that he adopted with his usual facility a hypothesis which appealed to his own sense of fitness and to his imagination.

CHAPTER XI

Fifty Years of England

Students who follow the course of English history during the eighteenth century become aware of far-reaching changes which come more clearly to notice as the third quarter of the century draws to a close. Looking backward, the historian recognizes these changes as having foreshadowed the birth of the modern world; for to them the eighteenth century, so long abused as a dreary waste among otherwise fruitful centuries, is "an Era of New Departure." No little of the importance of the man who is the subject of this volume lies in the fact that he was in spirit and practice a man of the new world but then coming to birth.

When John Wesley was born, England was a sleepy kingdom officially united not even with Scotland. When Wesley died, the British Empire was far on its destined way; if the Thirteen Colonies had been lost, India, Nova Scotia, and Canada were incontestably British. When Wesley was born, England was indeed a nation of shopkeepers; when the evangelist died, his country was the one industrial nation in a new world which was to be predominantly industrial. In the year 1703 the entire population of England did not equal that of modern London, and that population was centered primarily in the agricultural districts of the south. In 1791, when Wesley died, the population was leaping forward at a rate to frighten Malthusian minds; and sleepy villages were giving way to great cities, principally in the Midlands and the North, Liverpool, Manchester, Leeds, Sheffield, Birmingham. Even more important to remember are the intellectual changes which took place in these eventful years. In the first days of Queen Anne the medieval conception of a regulated world was yet the ruling idea of commerce, of government, of literature, of religion. In the days of George III "freedom" was the watchword of business and government, individualism was the new and insistent note of literature and religion.

How Wesley fitted into this changing scene may well be studied from the vantage point of the sixth and seventh decades of the century, for these decades saw the rise or development of the new movements in government, business, agriculture, population, literature, and religion. In 1763 the Treaty of Paris was signed, concluding the Seven Years' War and guaranteeing to England her conquests in America and India. From 1767 to 1779 came the three inventions which were to revolutionize the textile industry—Hargreaves' spinning jenny, Arkwright's water frame, Crompton's "mule." In 1765 Watt produced his first steam engine.

Industrial changes during the last quarter of the century were to transform even the appearance of England. The "dark, Satanic mills," which Blake and Ruskin were to hate, were springing up where had been only peaceful villages or unspoiled meadows. Cities grew where raw material could be had, for the new factory system required the presence of large numbers of laborers. The enclosure of common fields had been going on rapidly since the fifties because of changed agricultural methods which were making capitalistic farming profitable, and dispossessed cottagers were straggling into the new industrial towns to get work in the dark, ill-ventilated factories. The price which England was to pay for her industrial greatness was the wretchedness of cottagers despoiled of ancient rights to pig and cow and common, and misery and vice in the overcrowded cities where drink, disease, and poverty combined to create the shambles of Hogarth's pictures.

With economic change involving the breakdown of the old order went a change in men's minds. Voices were raised praising personal liberty as the only good gift of government; there were rumors that all men are created free and endowed by their Creator with certain inalienable rights. By 1776 the American colonies had formulated the political consequences of these beliefs in a historic document, while in the same year a Scottish economist, Adam Smith, published an almost equally momentous statement of their economic bearing. During these decades poets were beginning to revolt against the common sense and correctness of the Augustan Age, for the movement which brought back "warmth and colour" into English letters was essentially an individualistic protest on the part of those who were not afraid even of their own emotions. The modern world was to be ruled by modern men.

To all these changes the church was singularly unresponsive. Until after the American Revolution the colonies were under the religious direction of the Bishop of London, who added to his already heavy duties a desultory oversight of regions with which he was in no wise familiar. The Church of England made little effort to reach the groups of people driven to the cities by enclosures of farmlands or deprived of their livelihood by the factories. New cities in the industrial district received scant attention. Under the Whig bishops the church had become an adjunct of the state, a consummation for which the great church lawyer, Edmund Gibson, Bishop of London (1720-48), labored with uncommon zeal. Purged of her most zealous element by the secession of the nonjurors in the first part of the century, the church was finally cleansed of all but a parlor Jacobitism and made an innocuous branch of the government. As a result religious zeal was minimized and political conformity exalted.

The sentiment of many churchmen was that of Matthew Green "of the Custom-house,"

> But to avoid religious jars
> The laws are my expositors,
> Which in my doubting mind create
> Conformity to Church and State.

No more than his contemporaries did John Wesley appreciate the full significance of the changes which were going on about him; one would hardly expect him to produce doctrinaire discussions of, say, an economic movement which was not named until a century later. But there are ample evidences that he was aware of what was happening. In his writings, especially in his pamphlets on "the state of the nation," contemporary England is seen through the eyes of the man who perhaps knew it better than any other in the kingdoms. He had, as he himself said, "such opportunities of being informed as few persons in England have; as I see almost all the large towns in the kingdom, once in two years at least, and can therefore make those inquiries on the spot, as minutely as I please." If sometimes his description does not fit into modern reconstructions of history, his testimony is all the more valuable.

In 1773 Wesley deplored the starving of many people throughout the Isles, attributing the scarcity of provisions to several causes. Among these causes were distilling, luxury, and monopolies of farmlands. Squeezing out of small landowners was, he thought, "perhaps as mischievous a monopoly as was ever introduced into these kingdoms." But economic depression was a passing phase according to Wesley's testimony, for a few years later he wrote in most complimentary language of the prosperity of England.

His own observations convinced him of the falsity of that strange delusion which haunted so many minds during the latter part of the century, the delusion that England's population was declining. In 1778 Wesley expressed his opinion that the population had not grown less since 1759 and added: "I cannot but think there has been, within twenty years, an increase of more than an hundred thousand, in six cities and towns only; I mean, in London, Bristol, Birmingham, Sheffield, Manchester, and Liverpool." This increase, contrary to much contemporary and modern belief, was not confined to the towns. Houses were being built and the countryside improved. Wesley was little impressed with Goldsmith's lachrymose lines about sweet Auburn. Commented the Methodist:

I read in a very beautiful poem, of a "deserted"—what? province? county? metropolis? No—"village," somewhere on the Wiltshire Downs![1] Yet not quite deserted; for a gentleman who lives there informs me, he cannot learn it has had more inhabitants within these hundred years than it has at this day.

Progress in agriculture, manufactures, roads, and canals is constantly referred to in the *Journal*. One instance will illustrate. In 1774, two months before James Watt came there with his steam engine, Wesley visited the Boulton ironworks at Soho. The works Wesley thought to be "wonderfully ingenious, but the greater part of them wonderfully useless." Eight years later he was much impressed by the "high degree of perfection" which Boulton—he does not mention Watt—had reached in his foundry, which at that time employed about five hundred men, women, and children.

Far more important than any passing references to contemporary conditions is the way in which Wesley sought to meet what he conceived to be the needs of his time. His relations to the colonists may be dismissed for the moment while his work at home is called to mind. If one should plot the Methodist advance in England during Wesley's lifetime, the resultant map

[1] Modern scholars usually locate Goldsmith's "Sweet Auburn" in Ireland.

would be found to coincide with the shifts in population and the industrial changes of the period. The triangle which is formed by the three major points of Wesley's labors in England, London, Bristol, and Newcastle upon Tyne, incloses the chief industrial section of the country. For over a half century this man's work was centered in territory which was destined to be the heart of the industrial world. Methodist historians have plausibly explained this remarkable fact, as Wesley himself would unquestionably have done, by giving the credit to Providence.

Wherever he worked, Wesley strove first to save men's souls, then to save their bodies. The Holy Club had made much of charity, education, and personal ministration to the sick or imprisoned. When the first strictly Methodist societies were organized, it was required that those who retained membership in them should justify the same by "doing good to the bodies of men." In 1730 young Wesley was moved by the distress in Oxford, and he began depriving himself in order that he might have money to give away. Among other things, he wore his hair long to avoid the expense of the elaborate hairdressing expected of a gentleman. His own statement concerning his personal practice was as follows:

One of them [the Oxford Methodists, and he means himself] had thirty pounds a year. He lived on twenty-eight, and gave away forty shillings. The next year receiving sixty pounds, he still lived on twenty-eight, and gave away two and thirty. The third year he received ninety pounds, and gave away sixty-two. The fourth year he received a hundred and twenty pounds. Still he lived as before on twenty-eight; and gave to the poor ninety-two.

This must be appreciated with the fact in mind that Wesley was of an extravagant family and that he himself in his early years at college showed marked symptoms of the family trait. In later years Wesley received much from his books, although

173

his own salary of sixty pounds a year was often in arrears. But his charities were always equal to, and sometimes in excess of, his income. His friend Henry Moore estimated that in fifty years Wesley gave away more than thirty thousand pounds. The charity which Wesley practiced himself he enjoined upon his followers. They were to make all they could, save all they could, give all they could.

In addition to his charities Wesley attempted a more constructive philanthropy. His best efforts were in the dispensaries and the lending fund. The latter was a fund ranging from 30 to 120 pounds which for more than twenty years was administered for the relief of workmen who would otherwise have been forced to pledge their tools, and for the help of worthy tradesmen in need of immediate assistance. The money was lent without interest, usually upon the indorsement of some worthy man, and was to be repaid week by week within three months. There is little information as to the extent of this philanthropy, but an account of one conspicuous instance of its usefulness is preserved in the *Confessions* of the printer James Lackington. In his *Memoirs* Lackington spoke in no kindly way of the Methodists, but he later admitted that his success had been due to help which he received from them. This success was not small, since Lackington had an income of five thousand pounds and sold one hundred thousand volumes annually.

At Bristol, Kingswood, London, Leytonstone, and Dublin, Wesley inaugurated schools for the children of the poor. These were carried on according to his notions of child life, and he was at one with his age in supposing that children were, in the phrase of a later time, "little men and women." He himself had been impressed by the strict discipline of his mother and her orderly instruction. Besides, his theory of the guilt of all men in their "natural" state made him regard moral education as a very difficult and serious affair. Therefore the children were forbidden to play and urged to duplicate their elders' conversion experience.

As for their textbooks Wesley wrote the grammars and edited all the others, in order that the children might not be polluted by immodest or profane language. Little can be said as to the efficiency of these schools beyond the remark that "the crude character of educational method was probably no worse than that of most of the schools of the time."

Wesley's institutions designed to relieve distress were paralleled by other institutions in the eighteenth century. The lending fund, the dispensaries, the schools, were all duplicated by various organizations; and there is little reason to assign originality to Wesley in any of these. His significance for English philanthropy in this period lies largely in the fact that he made such work an integral part of the program of his societies. What the Church of England left to the state and to voluntary societies, Wesley made central in his own labors. Moreover, the work was carried on largely by the classes in actual touch with conditions demanding relief.

Wesley laid great stress upon personal ministry to the poor and organized in his societies a corps of Visitors of the Sick. The rules governing them will show the character of training which the visitors themselves received:

But it may not be amiss, usually, to begin with inquiring into their outward condition. You may ask, Whether they have the necessaries of life? Whether they have sufficient food and raiment? If the weather be cold, Whether they have fuel? Whether they have needful attendance? Whether they have proper advice, with regard to their bodily disorder? especially if it be of a dangerous kind. . . .

Together with the more important lessons which you endeavour to teach all the poor whom you visit, it would be a deed of charity to teach them two things more, which they are generally little acquainted with: industry and cleanliness.

Thus people were taught to relieve the wants of their own class, and one may speculate as to the possible effect of this in a country where relief of the lower classes had long been looked upon as a duty to be performed by the upper strata of society and not as the proper goal of the lower classes themselves.

In many respects Wesley was of the spirit of the new industrial era. His organization of the societies, his conception and administration of constructive charities, and above everything else, his impatience with outworn methods stamp him as akin to that child of the industrial Revolution, "the business man." To all ancient restraints Wesley returned the pragmatic answer of the new race. "My Lord," he had said to the learned Joseph Butler, Bishop of Bristol, "wherever I think I can do most good, there must I stay, so long as I think so. . . . But if I should be convinced in the meanwhile that I could advance the glory of God and the salvation of souls, in any other place more than in Bristol, in that hour, by God's help, I will go hence; which till then I may not do."

The individualism of Wesley's theology is recognized, although his insistence upon conversion and his appreciation of the emotional life have sometimes been condemned by the same voices which laud the new freedom of the politicians or grow husky in praise of the romantic movement in literature. Ruthlessly Wesley carried the dominant tenet of his century into his theology. Nowhere is this more evident than in the controversy that nearly wrecked the Methodist movement.

Many of the clergy of the Church of England, and practically all dissenters, were Calvinists, adherents to the stern faith that man is saved only by the irresistible grace of God, that his destiny is not his own, that he is clay in the Potter's hands. But in the sixteenth century Dutch burghers, rebelling against aristocracy in church and state, had shown favor to the doctrine of one Arminius, who had held the contrary, declaring men's ability to accept or reject the proffered mercy of God. In England, Ar-

176

minianism was associated with High Church, and Wesley's antipathy for Calvinism was because of his High Church theology.

Calvinism has not, as is sometimes said, tended to make its professors subservient to tyranny; on the contrary it has been the creed of some of the greatest rebels. But in essence such a doctrine does deny individual responsibility, does take away from man the humbling and heartening faith that he has some control over his own destiny, here and hereafter. And with any such doctrine Wesley would have no commerce. Nevertheless, for a time he did not consider the question as other than theological; and he did not spend time on theoretical quandaries.

But as early as 1740 dissension arose in Methodist circles over the doctrine of predestination. John Wesley at first simply took the ground that a Methodist might be either a Calvinist or an Arminian and that the question should not be agitated. When Charles forbade admission of one Acourt because he held Calvinistic views, John decreed that one's opinions were not to be questioned; all he asked was that a member should not trouble others by disputing. But trouble increased, until Wesley thought it necessary to speak. He did so by preaching in Bristol against Calvinism. In this sermon on "Free Grace," Wesley delivered himself with unusual vehemence against the conception of a tyrannical God:

This is the blasphemy clearly contained in *the horrible decree* of predestination! And here I fix my foot. On this I join issue with every assertor of it. You represent God as worse than the devil; more false, more cruel, more unjust. . . .

Oh how would the enemy of God and man rejoice to hear these things were so! . . . How would he lift up his voice and say, "To your tents, O Israel! Flee from the face of this God, or ye shall utterly perish! But whither will ye flee? Into heaven? He is there. Down to hell? He is there also. Ye cannot flee from an omnipresent, almighty tyrant. And whether ye flee or stay, I call heaven his throne, and earth his footstool, to witness against you, ye shall perish, ye shall die eternally. Sing, oh hell, and rejoice, ye that are under the earth! for God, even the mighty God, hath spoken, and devoted to death thousands of souls, from the rising of the sun, unto the going down thereof! . . . Let all the sons of hell shout for joy! For the decree is past, and who shall disannul it?"

Yea, the decree is past: and so it was before the foundation of the world. But what decree? Even this: "I will set before the sons of men, 'life and death, blessing and cursing.' And the soul that chooseth life shall live, as the soul that chooseth death shall die."

So far did he carry his belief in the freedom of the individual that even on the question which was considered crucial as between Catholics and Protestants—salvation by faith—the Minutes of 1770 spoke as follows:

1. Who of us is *now* accepted of God? He that now believes in Christ, with a loving, obedient heart.

2. But who among those that never heard of Christ? He that feareth God, and worketh righteousness, according to the light he has.

3. Is this the same with "he that is sincere"? Nearly, if not quite.

4. Is not this "salvation by works"? Not by the *merit* of works, but by works as a *condition*.

5. What have we, then, been disputing about for these thirty years? I am afraid, *about words*.

6. As to *merit itself,* of which we have been so dreadfully afraid: we are rewarded "according *to our works*." . . . How does this differ from *for the sake of our works?* And how differs this from *secundum merita operum,* as our works *deserve?* Can you split this hair? I doubt I cannot.

In response to the controversy raised by this minute Wesley "interpreted" it in the conventional terminology of justification by faith; but his essential convictions were without doubt set forth in the minute.

On the doctrine of predestination Wesley separated from his dearest friends. Whitefield was in America when John Wesley preached his sermon on "Free Grace" in 1740, but he immediately remonstrated by letter. Partisans attempted to raise trouble between the friends by distributing at the door of the Foundry, where Wesley was preaching, a broadsheet containing some remarks of Whitefield on the subject. When he arose to speak, Wesley held up the broadsheet and said that he intended doing with it as he was sure Whitefield would approve, tearing it up without reading it. Accordingly he tore his paper into bits, and the people did likewise with those which were in their hands.

The division between the Wesleys and Whitefield could not thus be averted. Some friends built Whitefield a tabernacle near Wesley's Foundry, and the two former comrades preached for a while, if not in opposition, at least in different camps. Whitefield would never have attempted to give form to his movement by organization if he had not fallen in with a woman of executive ability who supplied ambition and money for the purpose. Selina, Countess of Huntingdon, was converted and at once took Whitefield under her patronage. The evangelist was thus thrown into company where aristocratic doctrine was especially popular. At the countess' house in Chelsea, Whitefield preached to a discriminating audience of whom unbelievers such as Chesterfield and Bolingbroke were often members.

With the Countess of Huntingdon, Whitefield was also associated with Calvinistic clergymen who co-operated in spreading Methodism with a Genevan accent. The Honorable and Rev. Walter Shirley, cousin of the countess, was one of her noted preachers. Shirley, with his cousin, was connected with many of the princely houses of Europe and was brought to public notoriety in England by the unfortunate career of his brother, the Earl of Ferrers, whose trial and execution for a particularly cold-blooded murder was one of the celebrated cases in the latter half of the century.

Lady Huntingdon herself built chapels, purchased advowsons for evangelical clergymen of the Calvinistic persuasion, and in every way forwarded the cause. In the course of the work her followers came into inevitable conflict with Wesley's. During Whitefield's lifetime he and his two great comrades had only temporary estrangements. They preached in each other's pulpits and except for occasional lapses remained as of old. On September 29, 1770, Whitefield preached for nearly two hours in the open air at Exeter, New Hampshire. "You are more fit to go to bed than to preach," said a friend, before the evangelist began.

"True," replied Whitefield; then added, "Lord Jesus, I am weary *in* thy work, but not *of* thy work." The next day he died and was buried in Newburyport, Massachusetts.

Whitefield intended to be buried in his chapel in Tottenham Court, and he wished the Wesleys to be buried there also. "We will all lie together," he said; and he admonished his congregation: "You refuse them entrance here while living: they can do you no harm when they are dead." According to Whitefield's request John Wesley preached the funeral sermon in the Tottenham Court Chapel and also in Whitefield's tabernacle in Moorfields. His text was, "Let me die the death of the righteous, and let my last end be like his!"

Restrained during his lifetime by the friendship of the leaders, after Whitefield's death the storm broke. The "Minutes" quoted above were already in circulation, and the famous "Calvinian Controversy" began. Books, pamphlets, hymns, newspaper articles, which were the weapons of the antagonists, now seem barren and repulsive. The Rev. Augustus Montague Toplady, who was a brilliant controversialist, sometimes wrote like a costermonger. "Mr. Augustus Toplady I know well," wrote John to his brother, "but I do not fight with chimney sweepers. He is too dirty a writer for me to meddle with; I should only foul my fingers." Polemics in the eighteenth century naturally involved the versifiers. Few controversies called forth worse

examples of this sort. The Wesleyan position was attacked as
Roman Catholic.

> In vain for worse may Wesley search the globe,
> A viper hatched beneath the harlot's robe;
> Rome, in her glory, has no greater boast,
> Than Wesley's aims—to all conviction lost.

If Charles Wesley's missiles were no more soothing, they were
at least better jingles.

> *O Horrible Decree*
> Worthy of whence it came!
> Forgive their hellish blasphemy
> Who charge it on the Lamb.
>
> .   .   .   .
>
> [The doctrine he explains as follows:]
> The righteous God consigned
> Them over to their doom,
> And sent the Saviour of mankind
> To damn them from the womb;
> To damn for falling short
> Of what they could not do
> For not believing the report
> Of that which was not true.

This controversy divided the Methodists and many of their
sympathizers into two camps. Lady Huntingdon's chapels were
later licensed as dissenting chapels, and most of her clerical
helpers, choosing to remain in the Church of England, severed
formal connection with her, while Wesley continued to labor
to retain his followers within the church.

Wesley's marked affinities with the modern world to which
a dying century was to give birth must not be allowed to over-
shadow the fact that in some things he remained always a son

of the old order. He never gave over his autocratic rule of the societies. As late as 1779, when Wesley was seventy-six years old, one of the most popular of his preachers, Alexander M'Nab, openly defied his authority. M'Nab was preacher at Bath, and Wesley instructed him to allow an Irish preacher, unknown to M'Nab, to occupy his pulpit. M'Nab refused, alleging that he had been appointed by the conference, not by Wesley; and Wesley promptly deposed him. This difficulty, which a competent historian considered the most dangerous ordeal through which Methodism passed during the lifetime of its founder, was met by Wesley's calm statement, "As long as any preacher joins with me, he is to be directed by me in his work." Almost a decade later, when he was eighty-five years old, Wesley wrote to the trustees of a chapel at Dewsbury, who had refused to accept his method of "settling" chapels: "Therefore, if you will not receive them [Methodist preachers] on these terms, you renounce connection with your affectionate brother, John Wesley."

If in his direction of Methodism he was a despot, he was a benevolent one. He asked for results, not theories; and he persisted in his autocratic rule because he believed this the only way to achieve his purpose. Democracies he distrusted, and he brought over from the days of mercantilism and divine right a firm belief in discipline. To counterbalance Methodist individualism, he stressed social control by his classes and bands, by class leaders and helpers; nor did his enthusiasm for such control diminish with age. In 1778 he wrote to one of his preachers:

Dear Billy,—The soul and the body make a man; the Spirit and discipline make a Christian. . . . Insist upon the observance of all the society rules, by all the members of society; and on the observance of all (even the least) of the band rules, by all that meet in band. I give, for instance, no band tickets to any woman, who wears either ruffles or a high crowned cap.

182

The "Spirit and discipline"—his followers were to speak much of that liberty which is said to be of the Spirit, but Wesley combined in himself the new emphasis of his century on the freedom of the individual with the discipline which was of the essence of an older society.

CHAPTER XII

The Spirit of '76

IF ENGLISHMEN in the 1760's and '70's were only mildly aware of economic and intellectual changes, they were keenly alive to the problems raised by their American colonies. In this, as in other concerns of the century, Wesley shared the interests and often the views of the most intelligent of his contemporaries. His own relations with the colonies were of long standing, for he had been in America before most of the generation which took active part in the Revolution were born; for when Wesley was in Georgia in 1736, George Washington was only four years old, and George III was not born until 1738, the year of Wesley's return to England. However unpleasant his stay in Oglethorpe's colony, Wesley did not allow his opinions to be warped by his personal experiences; and he had retained a lively interest in America and American affairs. Since his own return from the colonies he had had reliable sources of information concerning them. His friend Whitefield had gone up and down the seaboard preaching and collecting for his orphanage. From 1768 Wesley had preachers in the colonies. The first Methodist chapel was built in New York in that year, and one of the preachers was a convert of Wesley, a Captain Webb, who had lost an eye on the Heights of Abraham. In 1769 two missionaries were sent out with fifty pounds as a gift to the American work. Two years later two others followed, one of them Francis Asbury, the greatest figure in the founding of American Methodism. Then in the very teeth of the storm Wesley sent out two more trusted preachers. "I let you loose, George," he wrote to one of them, "on the great continent of America. Publish your message in the open face of the sun, and do all the good you can."

During the years when the conflict was brewing, Wesley's great concern was to avoid war. To this end he exhorted preachers and people in America to labor for peace. On March 1, 1775, Wesley wrote to Thomas Rankin, one of his preachers in America, telling him that "there is now a probability that God will hear the prayer and turn the counsels of Ahithophel into foolishness. It is not unlikely that peace will be re-established between England and the Colonies." He also enclosed with this letter a missive to his preachers in America. His advice to them was to keep neutral:

You were never in your lives in so critical a situation as you are at this time. It is your part to be peace-makers, to be loving and tender to all, but to addict yourselves to no party. In spite of all solicitations, of rough or smooth words, say not one word against one or the other side. Keep yourselves pure, do all you can to help and soften all; but beware how you adopt another's jar.

At the same time Charles Wesley was writing to Rankin:

As to the public affairs, I wish you to be like-minded with me. I am of neither side, and yet of both; on the side of New England and of Old. Private Christians are excused, exempted, privileged, to take no part in civil troubles. We love all and pray for all with a sincere and impartial love. Faults there may be on both sides; but such as neither you nor I can remedy: therefore let us and all our children give ourselves unto prayer, and so stand still and see the salvation of God.

The situation in England was alarming to one who wished for peace. On the one side were extremists who cried out for

America and liberty. Wesley found throughout the two kingdoms a "huge majority of them, exasperated almost to madness." The conditions, he thought, were similar to those of
1640, when the people had been excited in a similar way, largely "by inflammatory papers, which were spread, as they are now,
with the utmost diligence in every corner of the land." On the
other side voices were raised in fanatical opposition to the claims
of the colonists. In March, 1775, Lord Sandwich made a speech
in the House of Lords, in which he spoke of the Americans
as "raw, undisciplined, cowardly men," and repeated a story to
the effect that at the siege of Louisburg the Americans had fled
at the sound of a cannon.

Between these two extremes was a body of moderate opinion,
favoring the claims of the colonies, but understanding that
those claims embodied only requests for constitutional rights
and not a demand for independence.

Although I love the Americans as men prizing and setting a just
value upon that inestimable blessing, liberty, yet if I could once
persuade myself that they entertain the most distant intention of
throwing off the legislative supremacy and great constitutional
superintending power and control of the British Legislature, I
should myself be the very first person . . . to enforce the power by
every exertion this country is capable of making.

Until the middle of June, 1775, John Wesley belonged to
the moderate group whose sentiments were thus expressed by
the Earl of Chatham. On June 14 Wesley addressed a letter to
Lord Dartmouth, a leading Evangelical and then secretary for
the colonies. On the next day he sent an almost identical letter
to Lord North. The burden of these letters was a plea that it
was not common sense for England to attempt force against the
colonies. The latter were "terribly excited." Only the preceding
week a man from Philadelphia had informed Wesley that as

low as "the Jerseys and Pennsylvania," the people were determined against the English measures. They thought that they
were fighting for liberty, and this would give them an advantage
over mercenary troops. As to such stories as Lord Sandwich
had told about "raw, undisciplined troops," Wesley himself had a story about "our valiant, disciplined militia." A
clergyman who had been on the spot had told him that at
Prestonpans—which Wesley dated 1716—a large body of
English militia was advancing when a boy in a neighboring
wood accidentally fired a fowling piece, causing the valiant
militia to run for their lives. There were internal dissensions
to reckon with, continued Wesley in his letters. Trade had de-
cayed, and provisions were dear, so that there were multitudes
of idle people in England, "ready for the first bidder." Such a
condition of affairs might be a punishment on England's luxury
and profaneness. But one thing was to be done. Let my lord do
what he can for peace. "For God's sake, for the sake of the King,
of the nation, of your lovely family, remember Rehoboam!
Remember Philip the Second! Remember King Charles the
First!"

With this ominous warning Wesley ended his letters. He was
pleading for one thing—peace. On the question of the justice
of the American cause he had made but one statement, but that
was significant. In the very first of the letter he had written:

I do not intend to enter upon the question whether the Americans
are in the right or in the wrong. Here all my prejudices are against
the Americans; for I am an High Churchman, the son of an High
Churchman, bred up from my childhood in the highest notions of
passive obedience and non-resistance. And yet, in spite of all my
long-rooted prejudices, I cannot avoid thinking, if I think at all,
these, an oppressed people, asked for nothing more than their legal
rights, and that in the most modest and inoffensive manner that
the nature of the thing would allow.

A few days after penning these lines John Wesley was engaged in abridging for publication a pamphlet which had been written three months before by Dr. Johnson, directed *against* the Americans. In this he affirmed that the supreme power of England had a legal right to lay any tax "for any end beneficial to the whole empire" upon the colonies, and that the trouble in America had been fomented by malcontents in England who were determined enemies of monarchy.

The causes which within a few days' time changed John Wesley from a defender of the American cause to a determined opponent deserve more attention than has been given them by writers intent only upon defending Wesley from the charge of plagiarism. The following explanation is put forward, not merely because the subject has often been passed over by biographers, but also because an appreciation of Wesley's motives is valuable for all who would comprehend the complexion of public sentiment in England in those June days.

Politically Wesley was one with the great body of the country clergy of his day; he was "an High Churchman, the son of an High Churchman." As such he had inherited a tradition of loyalty to the Crown which harked back to the Stuart theory of the divine right of kings. In spite of all the talk about liberty and the rights of Englishmen, the call of church and king was still potent among large groups, among whom were the Tory clergy. Charles Wesley did not speak only for himself when he prayed for a king "subject to none but Thee," and wrote of the king as "Thy great vicegerent here." When John Wesley was asked how far preachers should preach politics, his answer was that they should speak on political questions only when it was necessary to defend the king or his government. As he wrote to Lord Dartmouth, all his prejudices were against the Americans.

These prejudices he had overcome in the light of his information about the colonies and his honest belief in the sincerity of their claims. But his sympathy did not include armed rebellion. "If a blow is struck," he wrote Charles on June 2, 1775, "I give *America* for lost, and perhaps *England* too." Bad as the situation was on the first of June, there was still hope. The king prorogued Parliament May 28, with a statement to the peers that he had reason to expect the continuance of peace. But on June 13 Wesley had a letter from America telling him that there had been bloodshed. Four hundred regulars, so said the report, and forty militia had been killed. The news was of the Battle of Lexington, fought April 19. On the day that he received this news, Wesley wrote Thomas Rankin in America: "The sword is drawn. And it is well if they have not on both sides thrown away the scabbard." On the next day he hastened to write Dartmouth, pleading with impassioned words for some efforts toward peace.

Yet he retained his faith in the Americans. The letter informing him of the battle was from America, doubtless stating that side of the case. The first news of the battle from English sources reached England May 26, and more particulars came May 28; but the official version arrived in London only on June 10. There excitement was intense. The official report of General Gage was published in the Gazette the very evening that it arrived. George III, who on May 28 had declared that there were reasons to expect continuance of peace, now declared that the Americans must be *either* colonists *or* independent. But on the fourteenth Wesley seems not to have received this official account and wrote Dartmouth and North in the words quoted above.

The simple explanation is that for nearly three months Wesley had been in Ireland. From June 13 to 28 he was ill, part of the time confined to his bed at the countryseat of the clerk to the Irish House of Lords, where he was nursed by his host's Methodist wife and daughter. Here shortly after his letter to the ministers Wesley must have received the official report of the Battle of Lexington, for the account received in London on the tenth would normally reach Dublin a week later. Here also, it may be assumed, he met for the first time with Dr. Johnson's pamphlet *Taxation No Tyranny,* which had been published in London about the time that Wesley left for Ireland. Inflamed by the official report, which seemed to prove that the Americans were striking for independence, Wesley was prepared to be convinced by Dr. Johnson's fiery pamphlet. At once he began in characteristic fashion to abridge and edit it for publication. "As soon as I received more light myself," he wrote in explanation of his action, "I judged it my duty to impart it to others."

The government was almost pathetically grateful when Wesley issued his pamphlet *A Calm Address to our American Colonies.* Copies were handed out at metropolitan church doors, and representatives of the ministry called upon Wesley to offer the service of the government. But the opposition was even more vocal. The storm that broke upon the publication of the *Calm Address* is understandable only when one remembers the excitement of the time and the prominence of the author. A flood of pamphlets in answer came from the press. One of the most vigorous was from a Baptist minister in Broadmead, Bristol. Among other things he accused Wesley of having at a late election advised the Bristol Methodists to vote for the candidate who was favorable to the American cause, and with having recently recommended a book entitled *An Argument in Defense of the Exclusive Right Claimed by the Colonists to Tax Themselves.* Wesley denied that he had seen the book, whereupon the preacher proceeded to get two witnesses for his statement. A little later Wesley laconically answered that he now remembered the book. To a friend he wrote:

Dear James—I will now simply tell you the thing as it is. As I was returning from the Leeds conference one gave me the tract which you refer to, part of which I read on my journey. The spirit of it I observed to be admirably good; and I *then* thought the arguments conclusive. In consequence of which, I suppose (though I do

190

not remember it) I recommended it both to you and others; but I had so entirely forgotten it, that even when it was brought to me the other day, I coud not recollect that I had seen it. I am, etc.

JOHN WESLEY.

A writer in the *Gentleman's Magazine* who signed himself "Americus" put the substance of many attacks with a terseness not unworthy of Wesley himself. He wrote to Wesley:

You have forgot the precept of your Master that God and mammon cannot be served together. You have one eye upon a pension, and the other upon heaven,—one hand stretched out to the king, and the other raised up to God. I pray that the first may reward you, and the last forgive you!

In simple truth, Wesley had not changed his principles. He only changed his mind as to the motives of the Americans. His actions all the way through were entirely consistent with his political doctrines, and in his views he was at one with no inconsiderable part of middle-class England.

Of the charge of plagiarism little need be said. Such a charge moved Wesley very little indeed, for it was his common practice to abridge other people's works for the edification of his own constituency. His "Christian Library" was simply a "five-foot shelf of books" which he had abridged to make them suitable for his purpose. In this habit he had at least once run foul of a copyright. In 1745 he had had to pay the publisher Robert Dodsley fifty pounds for infringing the copyright of Young's *Night Thoughts* and some other works owned by Dodsley. In the case of *Taxation No Tyranny*, Wesley simply resorted to his usual practice; and neither he nor Johnson seems to have been in the least troubled by it. In 1797 the *Gentleman's Magazine* carried what purported to be an unpublished letter of Dr. Johnson to Wesley, the authenticity of which has not been challenged. After thanking Wesley for a copy of his *Notes on the New Testament,* which Wesley's sister Mrs. Hall had given him, Johnson referred to the *Calm Address*:

I have thanks to return for the addition of your important suffrage to my argument on the American question. To have gained such a mind as yours may justly confirm me in my own opinion. What effect my paper has had on the public I know not; but I have no reason to be discouraged. The lecturer was surely in the right who, though he saw his audience slinking away, refused to quit the chair while Plato stayed.

Having taken his position on the American question, Wesley allowed his Tory prejudices to have full sway in combating all opposition to the king and ministry. On July 31, 1775, he wrote his brother Charles concerning the rebellious tendencies of their Bristol printer, William Pine:

If he still, after my earnest warning, "every week publishes barefaced treason," I beg you would once more warn him in my name and in your own; and if he slights or forgets this warning, then give him his choice either to leave us quietly or to be publicly disowned. At such a time as this, when our foreign enemies are hovering over us and our own nation is all in a ferment, it is particularly improper to say one word which tends to inflame the minds of the people.

On October 17 he wrote to his brother: "I find a danger now of a new kind—a danger of losing my love for the Americans: I mean for their miserable leaders; for the poor sheep are 'more sinned against than sinning.'"

William Pine was not the only man in Bristol who was hot against the government. On February 3, 1777, Wesley went there to see for himself.

Hearing there was some disturbance at Bristol, occasioned by men whose tongues were set on fire against the Government, I went down in the diligence, and on *Tuesday* evening strongly enforced those solemn words, "Put them in mind to be subject to principalities and powers, to speak evil of no man." . . . On *Thursday* I wrote *A Calm Address to the Inhabitants of England.* May God bless this, as He did the former [his *Calm Address to our American Colonies*], to the quenching of that evil fire which is still among us!

In the latter pamphlet Wesley broke out in terms which were not likely to endear him to his brethren on the other side of the Atlantic:

Do any of you blaspheme God or the King! None of you, I trust, who are in connexion with me. I would no more continue in fellowship with those who continued in such a practice, than with whoremongers or Sabbath-breakers, or thieves, or drunkards, or common swearers.

On the fundamental doctrines involved in the discussions of American rights, Wesley took a view sharply distinguished from the doctrines then becoming fashionable. In this his position was not in accord with the trend of his century. The opinion of respectable sympathizers with the American Revolution was set forth by a prominent nonconformist minister, one Dr. Price, in *Observations on the Nature of Civil Liberty, the Principles of Government, and the Justice and Policy of the War with America.*[1] Price held the thesis that all men have a right to be self-governed and independent. Rousseau's favorite doctrine set forth in this fashion was as unacceptable to the Tory Methodist as was Rousseau himself. Wesley read *Emile* and thought the author the most "consummate coxcomb [who ever] saw the sun!" He was a misanthrope and a cynic, and the things which he said which were new were "lighter than vanity itself." "Such discoveries," observed Wesley, "I always expect from those who

[1] The popularity of Price's pamphlet may be judged by the fact that the preface to the first edition was dated February 8 (1776) and that to the fifth edition was dated March 12 of the same year.

are too wise to believe their Bibles." This whole theory of natural rights Wesley attacked at the source.

Wesley granted that men had a right to be self-governed and independent when no civil governments were in existence, but he asked, "When was that time, when no civil societies were formed?" He thought that there had been no such time since the Flood and appealed to history in support of his position. Did the people of England choose their governors before William the Conqueror? Did they choose King Stephen or King John? As to Charles I the "people" neither gave him his power nor took it away. Wesley, of course, repudiated the Commonwealth; Charles was executed by not even a tenth part of the people. In the same realistic fashion he dismissed the political fiction concerning the accession of William III, for the convention that summoned the Hollander was not the people of England. In actual politics, he contended, no one pretends that every human being has a right to govern. In republics women and men under twenty-one are excluded; in England those not freeholders or possessed of forty shillings a year could not vote. Such exclusion was certainly not in accordance with the doctrine of the "rights of man."

After depriving half the human species of their natural right for want of a beard; after having deprived myriads more for want of a stiff beard, for not having lived one-and-twenty years; you rob others, many hundred thousands, of their birthright for want of money!

Differing root and branch from the men who believed in "natural right," Wesley took a realistic view of the trouble with the American colonies. His summary of the causes of the rebellion is a careful and concise statement of the English case. He had at first in his *Calm Address* referred the genesis of the American trouble to malcontents in England who desired to foment difficulty in the kingdom. Two years later he had revised his opinion. As early as 1737, when his brother returned from Georgia to England and had been driven by a storm into the port of Boston, the New Englanders were looking forward to independence. This spirit was promoted by the vast increase of wealth in the colonies. America had kept up trade, in spite of the Navigation Acts, with almost every part of Europe and had increased its wealth by the gentle art of smuggling. "And it is notorious that one of the greatest dealers in this kind was the celebrated Mr. Hancock." Smugglers could not be convicted by an American jury, and as a consequence the customs of North America brought in only a pittance to the English government.

In regard to Hancock, Wesley had other plain words to say. He described the Boston Tea Party:

The famous Mr. John Hancock, some time since, brought into Boston a ship load of smuggled tea, at noon-day. Just then came in the ships from London, laden with the same commodity, which, by the removal of the former tax, they were now enabled to sell cheaper than him. What could he now do *pro patria?* . . . in plain English, not to lose by his cargo? All Europe knows what was done. . . . It was not so commonly known who employed them [those who threw the tea into the harbor], or paid them for their labour. To be sure, good Mr. Hancock knew no more of it than the child unborn!

Wesley had decided ideas on smuggling, as he had come into conflict with it, on the Devonshire coast in particular; and he did not hesitate to speak as plainly about American smuggling as he had spoken against Irish and English smuggling:

"What! Do you compare Mr. H[ancock] to a felon?" I do, in this respect: I compare every smuggler to a felon; a private smuggler to a sneaking felon, a pick-pocket; a noon-day smuggler, to a bold felon, a robber on the highway. And if a person of this undeniable character is made president of a congress, I leave every man of sense to determine what is to be expected from them.

The repeal of the Stamp Act gave the Americans the impression that they had the sympathy of a large number of people in England. The defeat of the French left America with nothing to fear from Canada. So the way was paved for them to seek separation from England. Yet the Americans talked of allegiance and said that they desired nothing but the liberty of Englishmen, and many people in England cordially believed them; "I myself for one," said Wesley. At last when America was well entrenched, "The talk of liberty was over: independency was the word."

When Wesley wrote *A Calm Address to the Inhabitants of England* (1777), he was sure that the Lord had at last smiled on the English in answer to a general fast which the king had proclaimed. The English forces had taken possession of Long Island and of New York, Fort Washington and Fort Lee. Wesley was moved to hope that even the atrocities of the Americans, "who drive men, women, and children into the wild woods in the depths of winter," and who burn down whole towns "without any regard for the sick or aged, that necessarily perish in the flames," were over.

Despite his attack upon the American cause, Wesley agreed in theory with his friend Dean Joseph Tucker, of Gloucester, who, though a Tory, was setting forth the theory that colonies were unprofitable, that trade would follow the most lucrative channels. If the Americans were free to do as they pleased, they would trade with England, because England could undersell other nations. England should not enter into a useless war to hold the colonies, but should drop them and promote commerce. This position was to be the position of Adam Smith and the new economic liberalism, and to this Wesley agreed. On December 26, 1775, he wrote:

But I say, as Dean Tucker, "Let them drop." Cut off all other connexion with them than we have with Holland or Germany.

Four-and-thirty millions they have cost us to support them since Queen Anne died. Let them cost us no more. Let them have their desire and support themselves.

Wesley's attitude on the American question was making his control of American Methodists impossible. His preachers in the colonies were suspected; only Asbury was able to remain at his post, and he was in hiding part of the time. Increasingly it became evident that Methodism in America would be independent of British control, either in the person of Wesley or of the Church of England. In 1779 some of the preachers in the southern colonies took it upon themselves to administer the sacraments without the authority of previous ordination. Before the close of the war Wesley was faced with the fact that the fifteen thousand American Methodists would not be content to be members of a religious society—they would have nothing less than a church.

CHAPTER XIII

Anacreon

On June 28, 1782, Wesley wrote in his *Journal*:

I entered my eightieth year; but, blessed be God, my time is not "labour and sorrow." I find no more pain or bodily infirmities than at five-and-twenty. This I still impute (1) to the power of God fitting me for what He calls me to; (2) to my still travelling four or five thousand miles a year; (3) to my sleeping, night and day, whenever I want it; (4) to my rising at a set hour; and (5) to my constant preaching, particularly in the morning.

The regimen to which Wesley attributed his vigor is illustrated by his diary[1] for the closing years of his life. This last diary begins December 1, 1782, and continues until October 24, 1790. The most significant disclosure which the day-by-day record makes is that until the end John Wesley lived as if he were yet a member of the Holy Club of Oxford. He rose at four in the morning, occasionally at three, to go about his duties, as methodically as if he were thirty instead of eighty. And his mind was as active as his body.

After he was eighty Wesley made two trips to Holland, his half-apologetic air betraying the fact that they were mainly in the way of being pleasure jaunts. On June 12, 1783, he sailed

---

[1] The diaries which Wesley kept during his entire life and which furnished the facts for his printed *Journal* have not all been preserved, but his private record of the last eight years is fortunately one of those which has escaped the fate of the diaries for the middle period of his life.

from Harwich, reading an *Account of Holland* during the crossing. In Holland he met many friends, among whom were Scottish and English ministers who opened their churches to the venerable itinerant. As almost forty-five years before, he was delighted with Dutch cities. He found Rotterdam "as clean as a gentleman's parlour." He admired the marble used for interior ornament and wondered why other nations had not copied this excellence. The women and children were beautiful, and their bland faces seemed to him to have "an inexpressible air of innocence." Nothing escaped his curious old eyes.

One little circumstance I observed which I suppose is peculiar to Holland: to most chamber windows a looking-glass is placed on the outside of the sash, so as to show the whole street, with all the passengers. There is something very pleasing to these moving pictures. Are they found in no other country?

Everywhere he was treated with such courtesy that he protested against the notion that Hollanders are "of a cold, phlegmatic, unfriendly temper. Not even the Irish are more affectionate." On July 4 he returned to London to look back on his trip with no little satisfaction. He wrote in his *Journal*:

I can by no means regret either the trouble or expense which attended this little journey. It opened me a way into, as it were, a new world; where the land, the buildings, the people, the customs, were all such as I had never seen before. But as those with whom I conversed were of the same spirit with my friends in England, I was as much at home in Utrecht and Amsterdam as in Bristol and London.

Three years later he paid another visit to Holland, again meeting with almost universal kindness and enjoying the little holiday among surroundings which appealed to his innate love of neatness and orderly living.

But all his admiration for another people could not separate him from his first love. Shortly after his return from his visit to Holland in 1783, he went to Oxford, perhaps to see if it did compare with the new country he had so much admired. So ran his *Journal* entry:

Observing narrowly the hall at Christ Church, I was convinced it is both loftier and larger than that of the Stadthuis in Amsterdam. I observed also the gardens and walks in Holland, although extremely pleasant, were not to be compared with St. John's or Trinity gardens; much less with the parks, Magdalen water-walks, &c., Christ Church meadow, or the White Walk.

He was yet "John Wesley, Sometime Fellow of Lincoln."

In February, 1784, Wesley met with his preachers to consider whether missionaries should be sent to the East Indies. The decision was that there was as yet no "providential opening" there. The next week after this conference Wesley spent an hour with Boswell's hero General Pascal Paoli. Wesley's admiration for the Corsican was unstinted, but he made characteristic comment to the effect that the general was happier in his retirement than in the midst of his victories. The life which Wesley's temperament as well as his Methodism made impossible for him, the seclusion of a scholar within the gray walls of Oxford, never ceased to haunt him.

On March 1 Wesley, then eighty-one years old, set out on a seven months' journey to the West of England, Scotland, and Wales. He preached incessantly, reproved the people for leaving off early-morning services, noted some good stories about dreams, and read Ariosto, Voltaire, and *Fingal*. But even in his hardened little frame there were signs of decay. The intense cold made him sick, and to a friend who urged him to visit America again, he replied sadly, "Nay, I shall pay no more visits to new worlds, till I go to the world of spirits."

Wesley was now approaching the culmination of a long struggle. Forty years before, his first conference had considered the question: "Do we separate from the Church?" The answer then and ever since had been, "No." A decade after the first conference John Wesley had replied to Charles's fears by refusing to worry about what would happen after his own and his brother's death; they would keep the Methodists in the church while they lived, come what might after their death. But Wesley had not left everything to chance, and as he now prepared to take final steps to secure the future of Methodism, the old man must have looked back across the years to recall his various attempts to "settle" his societies before he died.

In 1763 Erasmus, a bishop of the Greek Orthodox Church, had come to London; and Wesley, after investigating his credentials, had at least three of his preachers, John Jones, Samuel Staniforth, and Thomas Bryant, ordained by the Eastern prelate. Toplady stoutly asserted that Wesley himself sought ordination as bishop from the same source, but there is little to support the statement. Had opposition among the Methodists not arisen to the point that the preachers ordained by Erasmus were prevented from exercising their priestly functions, part of Wesley's problem would have been solved. His ordained helpers could have administered the sacraments and thus stopped the clamor for ordination on the part of the Methodist itinerants. Besides, there would have been younger ordained men to have carried on the work after the founder's death. But so intense was the feeling, stirred up partly by Charles, that this effort came to naught.

Other attempts to establish the societies had likewise failed. A league of evangelical clergymen, who were to disregard doctrinal differences in caring for the societies, was wrecked on Wesley's insistence that his preachers must have the right to preach anywhere, in accordance with his principle "the world is my parish." A plan to have a committee appointed from the preachers after his death to perform duties previously undertaken by Wesley, to propose, admit, exclude, and appoint preachers, also fell by the wayside. Wesley saw very quickly that his committee would be only a cause of confusion. For this scheme he substituted that of nominating a successor, who should assume the Wesleyan dictatorship after his death. Fletcher, of Madeley, whom Wesley selected, is popularly supposed to have been chosen only because of his saintliness and learning; but he may have appealed to Wesley because his character retained some of the marks of the soldier of fortune that he had been in his early life. Whatever the reasons for his nomination, Fletcher declined to undertake such a task, promising only to assist in every way possible if he and Charles should outlive John Wesley himself.

In the meantime Wesley had done everything he could to forestall secession. The assistants had positive instructions to exhort those who were brought up in the church to continue therein. They were further charged: "Set the example yourself; and immediately change every plan [he meant time of service, and so on] that would hinder their being at Church at least two Sundays in four." The houses were plain "preaching-houses" or "chapels"; they were not to be licensed as dissenting meeting-houses; but if persecution rendered it necessary to license them under the Conventicle Acts, then the license was to be for a Methodist, not a dissenting, chapel. Services in chapel were to be distinguished from the public worship of the church. "But some may say, 'Our own service is public worship.' Yes; but not such as supersedes the Church Service; it presupposes public prayer, like the sermons at the University."

But the fateful moment when the future of the societies must be settled could no longer be postponed. In spite of his vigor Wesley knew that his days were numbered. Nearly 200 preachers and 44,000 Methodists in Great Britain alone could not be left to the mercy of his assistants and the graces of a church which had neglected where it had not opposed them. Beside these, 15,000 Methodists in America were speaking with a new note of independence; and no amount of exhortation could reconcile them to a church which now scarcely existed in the new nation. Unless he was to desert utterly the thousands whom he had called into his societies, Wesley was compelled to provide some scheme to perpetuate his work.

But would such a step mean separation from the church? This was the problem which he had evaded thirty years before when Charles had ceased to be an itinerant preacher and had besought his brother to take some decisive action before the Methodists should drift too far from the church. The first point to be settled, if Methodist organization was to continue, concerned the appointing of preachers to the chapels. The heart of Wesley's system was his power to send whom he would where he would. Already the trustees of the chapels were protesting; they wanted to choose their own preachers. "We are no republicans," answered Wesley, "and never intend to be."

To secure the power of appointment from falling to the trustees, Wesley executed a "Deed of Declaration" in the High Court of Chancery which provided that a conference of preachers should have the powers formerly exercised by himself. The conference was to consist of one hundred preachers whom Wesley chose out of the nearly two hundred then in service, and was to be a self-perpetuating body. The choice of one hundred preachers, the "Legal Hundred," caused some heartburnings; and several preachers, including the two Hampsons, one of whom later wrote the first *Life of Wesley,* left the connection. But Methodism had a permanent organization.

Wesley's second step was more radical. The preachers had long clamored for ordination, and the call of American Methodists was now imperative, for with the failing of the English church in the colonies after the Revolution, the people were left without the sacraments. Wesley had long believed that he, as a presbyter of the Church of England, had as much right to ordain as any bishop; for the doctrine of apostolic succession he held to be no more than a fable. Nevertheless, he had tried every method to secure episcopal ordination for his preachers. When his scheme to use Erasmus failed, Wesley tried to get Bishop Lowth, the great Hebraist, then Bishop of London, to ordain a man for America; but Lowth refused. There seemed nothing left for Wesley but for him to act upon his convictions and himself lay hands on his preachers.

Having broached the subject of American work to Thomas Coke, a clergyman and a doctor of civil law, Wesley received a curious reply broadly hinting that Coke would like to go to America. This Wesley approved, but Coke was not satisfied. In face of the evidence one can hardly deny that Coke wanted to be Bishop Coke. Wesley had already noticed that Coke's "grand enemy" was "applause." Now Coke appealed to Wesley for some sufficient authority, since Francis Asbury was reported to have said that he would receive no emissary from Wesley. Coke asked that Wesley lay hands upon him to give him authority to ordain others. This Wesley finally consented to do, although he expressly stated that he was "consecrating" him as "superintendent" of the work in America.

Whatever Wesley intended, Coke meant to be bishop. He so referred to himself later when he tried to secure amalgamation of American Methodism with the Protestant Episcopal Church. But against the idea of making bishops Wesley revolted. He had taken the steps to set up a church in America, because the one logic which he followed in critical moments, the logic of circumstances, constrained him; but he would have nothing of a "Methodist *Episcopal* Church." Hence the following letter to Asbury:

But in one point, my dear brother, I am a little afraid both the Doctor and you differ from me. I study to be little: you study to be great. I creep: you strut along. I found a school: you a college! nay, and call it after your own names! [Cokesbury—Coke and Asbury]. . . .

One instance of this, of your greatness, has given me great concern. How can you, how dare you suffer yourself to be called a Bishop? I shudder, I start at the very thought! Men may call me a knave or a fool, a rascal, a scoundrel, and I am content; but they shall never by my consent call me Bishop! For my sake, for God's sake, for Christ's sake put a full end to this! . . .

Thus, my dear Franky, I have told you all that is in my heart. And let this, when I am no more seen, bear witness how sincerely I am Your affectionate friend and brother.

JOHN WESLEY

There is no need to review here the long technical controversy over the "validity" of Wesley's ordinations. Charles, upon hearing of his brother's action, was beside himself. His own High Church position he stated in verse:

> How easily are bishops made
> By man or woman's whim!
> Wesley his hands on Coke hath laid,
> But who laid hands on him?

Two weeks after the ordinations Charles wrote to his brother:

Near thirty years . . . you have stood against the importunate solicitations of your preachers, who have scarcely at last prevailed. . . . But when once you began ordaining in America, I knew, and you knew, that your preachers here would never rest till you ordained them. . . . Alas! what trouble are you preparing for yourself, as well as for me, and for your oldest, truest, and best friends! Before you have quite broken down the bridge, stop, and consider! If your sons have no regard for you, have some regard for yourself. Go to your grave in peace; at least, suffer me to go first, before this ruin is under your hand. So much, I think, you owe to my father, to my brother, and to me, as to stay till I am taken from the evil. I am on the brink of the grave. Do not push me in, or embitter my last moments. Let us not leave an indelible blot on our memory; but let us leave behind us the name and character of honest men.

To Charles's point, quoted from a statement of Lord Chief Justice Mansfield, that "ordination is separation," John returned no direct answer. He protested that he intended no separation, although he believed himself a *scriptural* bishop and uninterrupted apostolic succession a fable "which no man ever did or can prove." He insisted:

But this does in no wise interfere with my remaining in the Church of England; from which I have no more desire to separate than I had fifty years ago. I still attend all the ordinances of the Church at all opportunities; and I constantly and earnestly desire all that are connected with me so to do. . . . And this was what I meant seven-and-twenty years ago when I persuaded our brethren "not to separate from the Church."

But Charles was right; the ordinations were not to stop with the preachers for America. John Wesley was now persuaded to ordain for Scotland, where the Methodists had as little chance to receive the sacraments as in the New World. Having gone thus far, impelled by the necessities of concrete situations, he took the final step and ordained men for England. Some twenty-eight men in all were ordained by Wesley for Methodist work in the British Isles and in America.

Thus John Wesley prepared the way for separation, but with pathetic tenacity he yet clung to his dream. On May 11, 1788, he wrote to Henry Moore:

Still, the more I reflect the more I am convinced that the Methodists ought not to leave the Church. I judge that to lose a thousand, yea ten thousand, of our people would be a less evil than this. . . . Our glorying has hitherto been not to be a separate body.

Over the date, May 4, 1789, Wesley published a sermon on "The Ministerial Office," in which he proclaimed once more the character of his Methodism—a Methodism which was fast coming to exist only in his own mind:

> This is our peculiar glory. It is new upon the earth. Revolve all the histories of the Church, from the earliest ages, and you will find, whenever there was a great work of God in any particular city or nation, the subjects of that work soon said to their neighbours, "Stand by yourselves, for we are holier than you!" As soon as ever they separated themselves, either they retired into deserts, or they built religious houses; or at least formed parties, into which none was admitted but such as subscribed both to their judgment and practice. But with the Methodists it is quite otherwise: they are not a sect or party; they do not separate from the religious community to which they at first belonged; they are still members of the Church;—such they desire to live and to die. And I believe, one reason why God is pleased to continue my life so long is, to confirm them in their present purpose, not to separate from the Church.

The Methodists were not a sect; they must stay in the church —this is repeated until one suspects that for the old man the very words were an escape from reality. But Charles, passionate in his loyalty to the Church of England, was not deceived. He continued to quote the Chief Justice's opinion: "Ordination is separation." And Charles was right.

Charles, who had written that he was on the brink of the grave, had remained the eccentric poet, becoming if possible more of a High Churchman as he grew older. The ordinations aroused him to hot words, but nothing could break the strong bonds which bound together the two brothers. "We have taken each other for better for worse," Charles wrote to John, "till death do us—part? No; but unite eternally."

For many years Charles's home in London had been a place to which many beyond the circle of the Methodists loved to resort. Charles was held in high esteem by the musical world, Handel having set not less than six of his hymns to music. His sons were musical prodigies: the boy Charles was organist to the Prince of Wales, the future George IV; and Samuel gave earnest of his future fame on the same instrument. The best musicians of the time, among them Dr. Burney and Dr. Howard, the organist, were attracted to the two young players. A distinguished company was often present at their father's house in Marylebone to hear them play, frequently with an earl as accompanist. Once Dr. Johnson called and asked the boys to play for him. When they began, he picked up a book and read during the whole time that they played. "After which," wrote Samuel in his *Reminiscences*,[1] "he said, 'Young Gentlemen, I feel much obliged to you both for your Civility.'" John Wesley attended these concerts occasionally, to show that he did not think them wrong; but he found himself, so he said, somewhat out of place among lords and ladies. He loved "plain music and plain company best."

Charles Wesley, now nearly eighty years old, would ride about London, dressed in winter clothes even in summer, mounted upon "a little horse, gray with age." Sometimes he would come to Henry Moore's house in City Road and, leaving his horse in the garden, would enter, crying, "Pen and ink! Pen and ink!" When they gave him these, he would write down the hymn he had been composing, salute the family, give out a short hymn, "and thus put all in mind of eternity."

Perhaps even more bitter to the eccentric old poet than his brother's action in ordaining had been his son Samuel's step in entering the Church of Rome. Samuel had found favor in high Catholic circles, and the Duchess of Norfolk was chosen to break the news to the father; but if there was any hope that

---

[1] Samuel Wesley's manuscripts, including his *Reminiscences* and a number of letters, are in the British Museum.

the interest of one of the oldest houses in England would lessen the old man's grief, it was doomed to disappointment. When the Duchess urged various reasons for his son's actions, the aged poet broke in: "Say, 'the loaves and fishes,' madam! say, 'the loaves and fishes'!" But John Wesley wrote his nephew a kind letter. He pleaded with "Sammy," who had never been very religiously minded, not for his return to the Church of England, but that he should seek to "experience that inward change of the earthly, sensual mind, for the mind which was in Christ Jesus." "Whether of this Church or that, I care not," he wrote; "you may be saved in either, or damned in either; but I fear you are not born again; and except ye be born again you cannot see the kingdom of God."

For some time, in the spring of 1788, Charles was ill. His brother sent him from various places letters full of medical advice—a split onion to be put warm to the pit of his stomach, ten drops of elixir of vitriol in a glass of water, and, of course, electricity. But "primitive physick" could not avail against the attacks of old age. On March 29 Charles died at his London home. High Churchman to the last, he would be buried by none but a clergyman and nowhere but in consecrated ground. So he was laid in the churchyard in Marylebone. Wrote John to one of the clerical assistants:

'Tis pity but the remains of my brother had been deposited with me. Certainly that *ground* [he refers to the burying ground behind the City Road Chapel where he himself was to be interred] is *holy* as any in England, and it contains a large quantity of "bonny dust."

Owing to a delay in the mails, John Wesley did not hear of his brother's death in time to attend the funeral. He said little to indicate his grief, but two weeks later, when he tried to give out one of the greatest of his brother's hymns, "Come, O Thou Traveler Unknown," and came to the lines,

THE LORD'S HORSEMAN

My company before is gone,
And I am left alone with Thee,

his voice broke, and sitting down, he buried his face in his hands.

Of John Wesley's old age we have pictures from many hands.
John Hampson, who left the connection after the Legal Hundred
had been appointed, has left a classic description of Wesley in
his latter years:

The figure of Mr Wesley was remarkable. His stature was of
the lowest: his habit of body in every period of life, the reverse
of corpulent, and expressive of strict temperance, and continual
exercise, and notwithstanding his small size, his step was firm,
and his appearance, till within a few years of his death, vigorous
and muscular. His face, for an old man, was one of the finest we
have seen. A clear, smooth forehead, an aquiline nose, an eye the
brightest and most piercing that can be conceived; and a freshness
of complexion scarcely ever to be found at his years, and impressive
of the most perfect health—conspired to render him a venerable and
interesting figure. . . .
In dress, he was a pattern of neatness and simplicity. A narrow,
plaited stock; a coat with a small upright collar; no buckles at his
knees; no silk or velvet in any part of his apparel, and a head as
white as snow, gave an idea of something primitive and apostolic;
while an air of neatness and cleanliness was diffused over his whole
person.

In his old age his "venerable figure" impressed all who saw
him. In 1784, while Wesley was preaching in Scotland, a boy by
the name of Walter Scott heard him more than once. Thirty-
five years later Sir Walter Scott wrote to Robert Southey, then
writing his *Life of Wesley*, that he had heard Wesley preaching
from a chair in Kelso churchyard. Scott, too, spoke of the
Methodist's venerable figure. The novelist had remembered the
stories which the aged preacher told, and repeated one of them
for Southey's benefit. Scott remembered Wesley to have said:

"A drunken dragoon was commencing an assertion in military fashion, 'G—d eternally d—n me,' just as I was passing. I touched the poor man on the shoulder, and when he turned round fiercely, said calmly, 'You mean, *God bless you.*'" In the mode of telling the story he failed not to make us sensible how much his patriarchal appearance, and mild, yet bold, rebuke, overawed the soldier, who touched his hat, thanked him, and, I think, came to chapel that evening.

On October 15, 1790, the poet George Crabbe heard Wesley at Lowestoft. He noted his reverend appearance and cheerful air, and was particularly struck by the way in which Wesley quoted some lines wherein he substituted his own name for that of Anacreon:

> Oft am I by woman told,
> Poor Anacreon! thou grow'st old;
> See, thine hairs are falling all!
> Poor Anacreon! how they fall!
> Whether I grow old or no,
> By these signs I do not know;
> But this I need not to be told,
> 'Tis time to *live,* if I grow old.

But if Anacreon grew old, he did not cease from work. On January 22, 1791, Wesley wrote a friend, "I am half blind and half lame; but, by the help of God, I work on still." The very next month he visited the London society, to give them their quarterly tickets granting admission to the society meetings, as was his custom. His assistant would have dissuaded him from this task, but to no avail. The two, therefore, worked for three weeks "from early in the morning till late at night, until he had spoken to upwards of two thousand people."

On February 24 his diary ends abruptly. Wesley had already

given over keeping his accounts. On July 16, 1790, he had written in his expense book, with trembling hand:

N. B.—For upwards of eighty-six years [he probably meant sixty-eight] I have kept my accounts exactly. I will not attempt it any longer, being satisfied with the continual conviction that I save all I can, and give all I can, that is, all I have.

On the same day that the diary ended Wesley wrote his last letter, to William Wilberforce, already parliamentary leader for the abolition of slavery:

MY DEAR SIR,—Unless the divine power has raised you up to be as *Athanasius contra mundum*, I see not how you can go through your glorious enterprise in opposing that execrable villainy, which is the scandal of religion, of England, and of human nature. Unless God has raised you up for this very thing, you will be worn out by the opposition of men and devils. But if God be for you, who can be against you? Are all of them together stronger than God? O be not weary of well doing! Go on, in the name of God and in the power of His might, till even American slavery (the vilest that ever saw the sun) shall vanish away before it.

Reading this morning a tract wrote by a poor African, I was particularly struck by that circumstance, that a man who has a black skin, being wronged or outraged by a white man, can have no redress; it being a *law* in all our Colonies that the *oath* of a black against a white goes for nothing. What villainy is this!

That He who has guided you from your youth up may continue to strengthen you in this and all things is the prayer of, dear sir,
                    Your affectionate servant.

Already the writer had recalled the words of his aged father: "Time has shaken me by the hand, and death is not far behind." On the next day after writing to Wilberforce, Wesley was taken ill. He was tenderly cared for by friends, who watched his every movement and sought at once to gratify his wishes and to record all in their memory. On the day before he died the old evangelist sat up and sang his version of Isaac Watts's hymn "I'll praise my Maker while I've breath." He gave careful directions about his affairs, particularly enjoining that he be buried, as the law directed, in woolen garments. On the same evening, after vainly trying to speak, he cried out: "The best of all is, God is with us." During the night he repeated many times the first words of the hymn "I'll praise—I'll praise." At ten o'clock on the morning of Wednesday, March 2, 1791, he died without a groan or a sigh.

Careful directions in his will provided that there should be "no hearse, no coach, no escutcheon, no pomp, except the tears of them that loved me." Six pounds were left for six poor men who should carry him to the grave. His friends followed his directions as best their spirits would allow. After lying in state in the chapel at City Road, hung with black at an expense which would have wounded the soul of its builder, the body was laid away in the unconsecrated ground at the rear of the chapel. Six poor men carried him to his grave, and one of his preachers read the service with but one change in the ancient form. When he came to the words of the committal "forasmuch as the spirit of our deceased *brother*," he paused and then read, "our deceased *father*," in a voice scarcely heard above the sobs of the congregation.

That the Methodist movement survived in England was due to the legal settlement which Wesley had given in the Deed of Declaration. For at once upon the founder's death disputes arose: trustees of chapels demanded their "rights" in appointing preachers; and Henry Moore, Coke, and Whitehead began wrangling over the disposition of Wesley's papers, of which they were executors. The latter dispute was the more intense, since John Hampson was publishing his memoirs of Wesley, which had been written before the great Methodist's death. Not only was Hampson thus anticipating a profitable market, but he was treating his subject as very great, but very human; and of the latter most of the preachers would have none. At last they could picture Wesley as they would have the world see him, and to make assurance sure, honest John Pawson was soon sorting his master's papers in the City Road house. "The greater part of the papers," he explained later, "were old good-for-nothing letters—not a few of which ought never to have been seen by anyone but himself, and which I wonder he had not destroyed." What Wesley had failed to do, the cautious Pawson did for him. And the chimney of the modest home in City Road carried away the smoke from these "old good-for-nothing papers," including Wesley's Shakespeare with annotations in his own neat hand.

The men who survived to fight the battle of Methodism were good men, many of them capable and intelligent; and within a few years they had built a church—built, it must be said, on foundations laid by John Wesley himself. But the catholic-minded man, who had dreamed of a new world in which men might adventure in the spirit without clash of creed or order, was dead; and what he would have thought and said of the works of his successors, no one will ever know.

Index

215

INDEX

217

INDEX

Scientific views, Wesley's, 151, 161-67
Scilly, Isles of, 91
Scotland, 138-40, 200, 206, 210
  Edinburgh, 140
  Glasgow, 138-39
Scott, Sir Walter, 210-11
Secker, Thomas, Archbishop of Canterbury, 157
Serious Thoughts on the Earthquake at Lisbon, 136
Sermons, 55
Seven Years' War, 135, 147, 169, 196
Sharp, John, Archbishop of York, 18
Sheffield, 172
Sherlock, Thomas, Bishop of London, 135-36
Shirley, Walter, 106, 179
Smith, Adam, 170, 197
Smith, John. *See* Secker, Thomas
Smollett, 155
Smuggling, 110-11, 195
Societies, Methodist, 107-10
Societies, religious, 107
Society for the Promotion of Christian Knowledge, 35
Society for the Propagation of the Gospel in Foreign Parts, 41, 42
Southey, Robert, 23, 120, 132
Spectator, The, 30
Spenser, 30, 31, 154
Standard Sermons, 152
Staniforth, Samuel, 201
Stanton, 31
Survey of the Wisdom of God in the Creation, A, 151, 161-67
Swift, Jonathan, 31
Sydenham, Thomas, 158, 159

Taxation No Tyranny, 188, 189-92
Tea drinking, 113-14
Theology, nature of Wesley's, 152-53
Tiverton, 65
Tomo-chachi, 47
Toplady, Augustus, 152-53, 180, 201
Trinity College, 200
Tucker, Dean Joseph, 196

Vazeille, Mrs. Mary. *See* Wesley, Mrs. John

Viney, Richard, 67
Violence against Methodists, 101-6
Voltaire, 200

Wales, 89, 100
Walpole, Horace, 80, 136
Walpole, Sir Robert, 23
Walsh, Thomas, 120
Washington, George, 184
Watt, James, 172
Webb, Captain, 184
Welch, Mrs., 44, 49, 50
Wesley, Charles, 17, 29, 42, 62, 64, 72, 126, 128, 129, 130, 143, 144, 145, 146-47, 185, 188, 201, 203, 205-9
  arrest, 93
  at Christ Church, 33, 34
  death, 209
  in Frederica, 49-52
  hymns, 82-83
  jingle on Calvinism, 181
  marriage, 129, 130, 147
  preaching, 83, 91, 104, 135, 146
Wesley, Charles, Jr., 208
Wesley, Emilia, 17, 28
Wesley, Hetty, 17, 32
Wesley, Mrs. John, 129-34
Wesley, Kezziah, 17
Wesley, Martha, 17
Wesley, Mary, 17
Wesley, Samuel, Jr., 17, 20, 23-24, 33, 39, 40, 65, 66, 84-85, 95
Wesley, Samuel, Sr., 15-24, 27, 32, 36-37, 38-39, 40, 93, 149
Wesley, Samuel (son of Charles), 208-9
Wesley, Susannah, 17, 18, 19, 27, 37, 39, 114, 149
Wesley, Susannah (sister of John Wesley), 17
Westminster School. *See* London
Wheatley, James, 104
Whitefield, George, 33-34, 37, 62, 73-74, 76, 77-80, 83, 84, 98, 101, 136, 147, 178, 179, 180, 184
Whitehead, John, 213
Wilberforce, William, 212
William III, 20, 194

219